YOUTH SOCCER DRILLS

Jim Garland, MS

Physical Education Instructor
North Harford Elementary School, Pylesville, Maryland

Coordinator of Motion Concepts Soccer Camps

Human Kinetics

Library of Congress Cataloging-in-Publication Data

Garland, James, 1948-
    Youth soccer drills / James Garland.
      p.   cm.
    ISBN 0-88011-528-9
    1. Soccer for children--Training. I. Title.
    GV944.2.G37   1996
    796.334'083--dc20   96-8064
                                                      CIP

ISBN: 0-88011-528-9

Photos: pp. 7 and 49 © Terry Wild Studio; pp. 77, 127, and 145 courtesy of James Garland; p. 181 © CLEO Freelance Photo; p. 199 © Connie Springer.

Acquisitions Editor: Ken Mange; **Developmental Editor:** Julia Anderson; **Assistant Editors:** Jacqueline Eaton Blakley and Sandra Merz Bott; **Editorial Assistant:** Coree Schutter; **Copyeditor:** Bob Replinger; **Proofreader:** Karen Bojda; **Graphic Designer:** Judy Henderson; **Graphic Artist:** Kathy Boudreau-Fuoss; **Photo Editor:** Boyd LaFoon; **Cover Designer:** Jack Davis; **Photographer (cover):** F-Stock/David Stoecklein; **Illustrator:** Susan Carson; **Printer:** United Graphics

Human Kinetics books are available at special discounts for bulk purchase. Special editions or book excerpts can also be created to specification. For details, contact the Special Sales Manager at Human Kinetics.

Printed in the United States of America   10 9 8 7 6 5

Human Kinetics
Web site: http://www.humankinetics.com/

United States: Human Kinetics, P.O. Box 5076, Champaign, IL 61825-5076
1-800-747-4457
e-mail: humank@hkusa.com

Canada: Human Kinetics, 475 Devonshire Road, Unit 100, Windsor, ON N8Y 2L5
1-800-465-7301 (in Canada only)
e-mail: humank@hkcanada.com

Europe: Human Kinetics, P.O. Box IW14, Leeds LS16 6TR, United Kingdom
+44 (0)113-278 1708
e-mail: humank@hkeurope.com

Australia: Human Kinetics, 57A Price Avenue, Lower Mitcham, South Australia 5062
(08) 82771555
e-mail: humank@hkaustralia.com

New Zealand: Human Kinetics, P.O. Box 105-231, Auckland Central
09-523-3462
e-mail: humank@hknewz.com

Contents

Chapter 3   Passing and Collecting Drills   **77**

Chapter 4   Heading Drills   **127**

Acknowledgments

To all my friends who helped either directly or with encouragement during this project, I thank you.

Thanks to all the clinicians, fellow teachers, and coaches who have helped educate me in the game of soccer.

A special thanks goes to Mr. Cloyd George Wagner, my high school soccer coach, who always made the game fun and taught me lessons of life that will always be with me when working with children.

To Dr. Donald Minnegan, Towson State University, thank you for sharing your knowledge.

And finally, to one of the most professional people I have ever known, Sharon Mitchell, thank you for all the hours spent typing, retyping, and printing. Without you, this would not have been possible.

Over the years, I have had the pleasure of working with thousands of children. Some were gifted athletes; some were gifted in other ways. All of them were special. Two of these children were, are, and will always be the most special to my wife, Pat, and me.

They have filled our hearts with unforgettable memories that we will cherish forever. They will not fully understand how much it has meant to have the opportunity to spend so much time with them, as their playmates, until they have children of their own.

To my sons, Casey and Matthew, this book is dedicated to you. Thank you for being my greatest teachers.

Introduction

When I was a child, I loved playing. I was the kind of kid who hated rainy days and got angry when the sun went down in the evening. I still do. This meant playing would have to wait until another day. I was active, very active. I'm still active. Being still was for someone else. Being still meant being bored. None of that for me.

As I grew into adulthood and considered future employment, I knew I wanted two things: to stay active in sports and to help young people experience the same joys I had while at play. Being an elementary physical education teacher and coach was a natural fit for me. I've been teaching for almost 30 years now and I've coached from clinic-level teams through high school boys' varsity sports. In that time I've discovered two things about working with kids: They want to have fun, and if they don't understand what you're talking about, it's probably not their fault.

When working with children as a physical education teacher and coach, I've tried to remember how I felt as a child. I remember how much I hated listening to a coach talk for 20 minutes and then getting to play for only 10 minutes. Standing in long lines waiting for a turn during drills absolutely frazzled me.

These thoughts helped inspire me to write this book. I wanted to give youth soccer coaches a resource filled with activities that are easy to explain and fun, keeping even the most active child satisfied. The drills I selected for this book meet these criteria. Besides providing drills to improve skills, I have heavily emphasized movement concepts to help improve the quality of players' movements. I have designed these drills for use by coaches of youth players 5 through 12 years of age. Players' parents and physical education instructors will also find this a handy reference.

The book is divided into seven chapters. It begins with a chapter on space and movement that discusses open, closed, personal, and general space. These ideas are integrated with concepts of vision, direction, speed, and level into drills that promote the development of efficient movement. Chapters 2 through 5 offer drills dealing with skill acquisition. Drills are organized in a progression from least to most challenging. Drills that are least challenging will require less movement. Players often learn skills more quickly by practicing from a stationary position. As players become more successful, drills become more challenging. The coach can introduce movement, change the responsibility of players, or restrict time, space, or touches. The coach can add defensive pressure, beginning with subtle pressure and progressing to gamelike pressure. These chapters include drills that develop skills in dribbling, passing, collecting, heading, and shooting. The book does not include drills to develop the special skills of goalkeepers. Instead, the book focuses on developing space, movement, and skill concepts for field players.

Chapters 1 through 6 include activities for individual, partner, and small-group drill work. Many drills contain more than one performance level. The higher the level, the more difficult the drill. Factors influencing the difficulty of the drill will vary and may include the addition of players as defenders, changing space requirements, combining movement with skills, and so on.

Chapter 6, "Game Progressions," discusses a plan for implementing structured games according to a player's readiness. The chapter identifies the concepts that the coach can present at the 3-versus-3, 3-versus-3-plus-goalkeeper, 7-versus-7, and 11-versus-11 levels. Chapter 7, "Using Drills in Practice," offers information about practice organization and includes sample practice plans for 5- to 7-, 8- to 10-, and 11- to 12-year-old players.

A drill finder is included to help make the drills more user friendly. The drill finder indicates the skills and concepts highlighted by the level of defensive pressure and the number of players in each drill. To use the drill finder, coaches should select the skill or concept they are interested in from the left column. The column headings on top indicate the type of defensive pressure presented in the drill. The columns on the bottom indicate the number of players in the drill. For example, a coach can look at the drill finder to locate a drill that would help improve dribbling skills for small groups with no defensive pressure. The drill finder shows that drill 21 would meet these requirements.

Coaches using this book will benefit greatly. They can help their players move more efficiently by using the drills concerning direction, speed, and level. Coaches will benefit by having a resource that will guide them toward a logical order of teaching skills and concepts. They will improve safety and reduce collisions during practices and games by using the information about movement concepts. In addition, coaches will benefit by developing a better understanding of what concepts they should present at each age level.

The book is not all-inclusive. Coaches should feel free to substitute some of their favorite drills where appropriate in the progression.

Many of the activities included in this book are original ideas, while I collected some by observing other coaches, clinicians, and teaching professionals.

I encourage all coaches to have fun using this book. Your players will be grateful and will never have to say the sun went down before they got their turn.

Drill Finder

Concepts	No defense			Subtle defense			Gamelike defense		
Dribbling	27	21	20, 22, 23, 25	27	26	24	27, 28, 29, 30	31	18
Passing and collecting	33, 34, 39, 45, 46	35, 36, 37, 38, 40, 41, 42, 44	32, 43		47, 48, 49			50, 51, 53, 54	52
Heading	56	57, 58, 59	55		60			61	
Shooting	62, 64, 65, 70	63, 66, 67, 68, 69, 71, 72		64, 65, 75	58, 59, 73, 74, 76, 77			74	
Space	56	1, 2	3, 4						
Movement	10, 11, 12	15	8, 9, 13, 16, 17			19	14		18
Vision			5, 6, 7						
Number of players	Single/ partner	Small group	Large group	Single/ partner	Small group	Large group	Single/ partner	Small group	Large group

Space Concepts and Movement Drills

C oaches, assuming that players know how and where to move when playing soccer, often neglect to train space and movement skills in favor of drilling skills like kicking, heading, and so on. This is unfortunate because to move with confidence and avoid collisions, players must understand space and movement.

Space concepts deal with *where* to move on the field. Training should include the concepts of open, closed, personal, and general space:

- **Open space** is where no objects (players) occupy an area.
- **Closed space** is an area occupied by one or more players.
- **Personal space** is an area immediately surrounding a player.
- **General space** is the entire area in which a player is allowed to function.

Movement concepts deal with *how* players negotiate space. Developing movement concepts includes training to develop vision, direction, speed, and level:

- **Vision** refers to looking in the direction of movement while using scanning techniques to improve peripheral vision.
- **Direction** refers to the ability to maintain or change pathway.
- **Speed** refers to the ability to change the rate of motion.
- **Level** refers to the position of a player's body in relation to the playing surface, such as jumping (high level) and sliding (low level).

The drills in this chapter develop space and movement concepts progressively. They begin with demonstrations concerning open and closed space. These are the fundamental concepts that guide much of the decision-making process concerning where to move and where to play the ball next. I have placed these demonstrations first in the progression primarily as a safety concern; the drills will help reduce collisions.

Personal- and general-space demonstrations are next in the progression. These are essential in helping to achieve field balance and avoid clustering of players. Visual training follows next, although it is certainly intertwined with demonstrations on open, closed, personal, and general space. The visual-training drills are presented to help develop awareness of the need for good visual habits that include breaking eye contact with the ground and scanning techniques. These habits will improve a player's field vision. Next in the progressions are elements of movement that help players to create or deny space. They include direction, speed, and level. Players can create space (move to open space away from other players) or deny space (move toward other players to close space) by changing directions, speeds, and levels more efficiently than their opponents. All the progressions are presented developmentally, gradually increasing the expectations for speed of execution.

Many of the drills do not initially use a ball. In this way players gain confidence moving without having to control a ball. As players demonstrate competency with movement, add a ball to increase the challenge.

1 Open-Space Demonstration

PURPOSE

To help players recognize how easy it is to move through unoccupied spaces. Use this demonstration to build a base of knowledge about the use of space and refer to it in later teachings.

EQUIPMENT

One ball, two game markers

TIME

Five minutes

PROCEDURE

Level 1

1. Have players huddled in a group.
2. Place two markers on a line about 10 yards apart.
3. Ask one player to stand by one of the markers.
4. Ask that player to walk to the other marker (see figure).

Level 2

1. Repeat procedures 1 and 2 from level 1.
2. Ask one player to stand by one of the markers with a ball.
3. Ask that player to dribble the ball to the other marker.

Level 3

1. Repeat procedures 1 and 2 from level 1.
2. Ask one player to stand by one of the markers with a ball and another player to stand by the other marker.
3. Ask the player with the ball to pass the ball to the teammate who is standing by the other marker.

Open-Space Demonstration

10 yd

KEY POINTS

You have demonstrated how uncomplicated it is to move, dribble, and pass through open space. Youth players will develop an understanding of space more thoroughly when you give a visual demonstration. Refer to this demonstration often when explaining effective use of space in training and game situations.

Related Drill   2

2 Closed-Space Demonstration

PURPOSE

To demonstrate how impossible it is to move, dribble, and pass through closed spaces.

EQUIPMENT

Two game markers, one ball

TIME

Five minutes

PROCEDURE

Level 1

1. Have players huddled in a group.
2. Place two markers on a line about 10 yards apart.
3. Ask player A to stand by one of the markers.
4. Ask player B to stand on the line at a point midway between the markers.
5. Ask player A to walk on the line to the other marker.

Level 2

1. Repeat procedures 1 through 4 from level 1, except player A has a ball.
2. Ask player A to dribble the ball to the opposite marker without going off the line (see figure).

Level 3

1. Repeat procedures 1 through 4 from level 1, except player A has a ball.
2. Ask player C to stand by the unoccupied marker.
3. Ask player A to pass to player C.

Closed-Space Demonstration 2

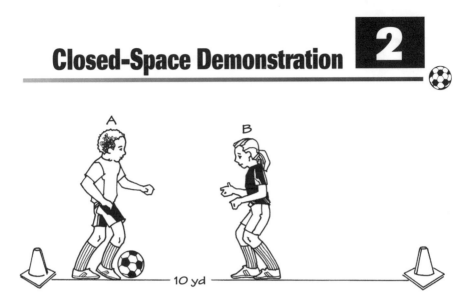

KEY POINTS

At level 1 player A will find this task impossible because player B, who has closed the space between the two markers, has blocked his pathway. At level 2 player A will not be able to dribble the ball through the space closed by player B. At level 3 player A will not be able to pass the ball through the space closed by player B.

Developing an understanding of open versus closed space should be a top priority for youth players. Give them this visual demonstration of how impossible it is to move without the ball, to dribble, or to pass through closed spaces. Refer to this demonstration when players begin clustering, colliding with teammates or opponents, or dribbling and passing into closed spaces. Explain to them the alternative, which is, of course, to use open space.

Related Drill   1

3 Personal-Space Demonstration

PURPOSE

To help develop an understanding that personal space is the space that immediately surrounds players and is affected by player movement.

EQUIPMENT

Nine game markers

TIME

Five minutes

PROCEDURE

1. Place five players each into four grids, each five yards by five yards. Number the grids 1 through 4.
2. Ask the players to move freely through their grids (see figure).
3. If a player touches another player, he is frozen.
4. Ask players from grid number 2 to join the players from grid number 1 and the players from grid number 3 to join the players from grid number 4.
5. At this point, all frozen players become unfrozen and rejoin the other players.
6. Ask the players to move freely in their grids for about 30 seconds.
7. Finally, have all of the players move to grid number 1.
8. Ask the players to move freely for about 30 seconds reminding them not to touch anyone as they move.

KEY POINTS

As the players move in a grid with only four other players, maintaining their personal space should not be challenging. As the

Personal-Space Demonstration

number of players in a space increases, movement becomes more difficult. When all the players are moving in a small space, it becomes almost impossible to maintain or not invade someone else's personal space. This drill can serve as a visual reminder for players during scrimmages and games how difficult movement becomes when they cluster. Hopefully, the result will be better spacing and less swarming so that players can maintain personal spaces.

Related Drills   1, 2, 4

General-Space Demonstration

PURPOSE

To help develop an understanding that general space is the entire area in which a player can function and that within this general space, larger spaces are easier to negotiate than smaller ones.

EQUIPMENT

Eight game markers

TIME

Five minutes

PROCEDURE

1. Have all players scattered in a grid identified by four game markers approximately 20 yards apart.
2. Ask them to move freely through the entire grid.
3. Expand the size of the grid to 50 yards by 50 yards.
4. Ask the players to move freely through the larger grid.
5. After the players move in both grids, discuss with them in which grid they found it easier to move.

KEY POINTS

The personal-space demonstration showed how increasing the number of players in a space affected a player's personal space and movement. This drill demonstrates how increasing the size of the space makes player movement easier because there is more time to make decisions about changing direction, speed, and level. Players should recognize that by using all the spaces within the

General-Space Demonstration

general space properly they can maintain field balance and move more freely.

Related Drills   1, 2, 3

Vision Training

PURPOSE

To develop good visual habits, which include breaking eye contact with the ground and scanning techniques.

EQUIPMENT

Four game markers

TIME

Five minutes

PROCEDURE

1. Position players in a scattered formation in a 20-yard-by-20-yard grid (see figure).
2. In a standing position, players lift first their right knees, left knees, look right, look left.
3. Players do this in a rhythmical four-count chant, verbalizing each part out loud.
4. Do several repetitions and then change the pattern.

Other patterns might include look right, look left, lift right knee, lift left knee; lift right knee, look right, lift left knee, look left; or lift left knee, look left, lift right knee, look right.

KEY POINTS

Some players move with their eyes focused on the ground. They are very susceptible to injury because of the possibility of colliding with other players whom they do not see. This drill includes looking left and right in a movement pattern executed within a player's personal space. This enables the player to practice vision techniques without the fear of collisions.

Related Drills   6, 7

Vision Training

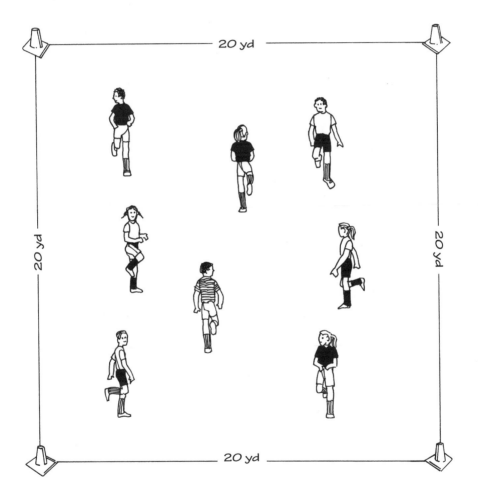

6 Stationary Vision Training With a Ball

PURPOSE

To help develop players' ability to use good visual habits while in possession of the ball. Good visual habits include breaking eye contact with the ball and scanning techniques.

EQUIPMENT

One soccer ball for each player, four game markers

TIME

Five minutes

PROCEDURE

1. Scatter players in a 20-yard-by-20-yard grid.
2. Each player stands with a ball in his or her hands (see figure).
3. Using a four-count rhythm, players, with arms extended, lift left knee to touch the ball held in both hands, then right knee, look left, look right. Players should verbalize this sequence as they repeat it several times.
4. Ask players to place the ball on the ground.
5. Have the players touch the top of the ball with the right foot, left foot, look left, look right.

KEY POINTS

Insist the players use a four-count rhythm and break eye contact with the ball during the sequence. As players progress, they will improve their vision and balance. Challenge them by using variations that might include striking the ball with various body parts including the head, chest, inside of knee, outside of knee, instep of foot, and outside of foot. Encourage players to develop pat-

Stationary Vision Training With a Ball

terns in which they must break eye contact with the ball after one or two touches. Do this training from a stationary position before allowing players to move with the ball. Players who move with a ball but have not learned to break eye contact with it and scan are more susceptible to collision.

Related Drills   5, 7

Moving Vision Drills

PURPOSE

To help develop good visual habits when negotiating space with and without the ball.

EQUIPMENT

One soccer ball for each player, four game markers

TIME

Five minutes

PROCEDURE

Level 1

1. Scatter players in a 30-yard-by-30-yard grid (see figure).
2. On the coach's signal, players move freely throughout the grid by walking to a four-count rhythm.
3. Players take one step with the left foot, one step with the right, one step with the left again, looking left as they step, and one step with the right looking right as they step.
4. Players verbalize the movement, chanting left, right, look left, look right.
5. Repeat, jogging.

Level 2

1. Repeat level 1 procedures while using a ball.

KEY POINTS

Movement affects a player's vision. You must train players to look constantly in the direction they are moving and scan right and left so that they can negotiate space efficiently. Practice this be-

Moving Vision Drills **7**

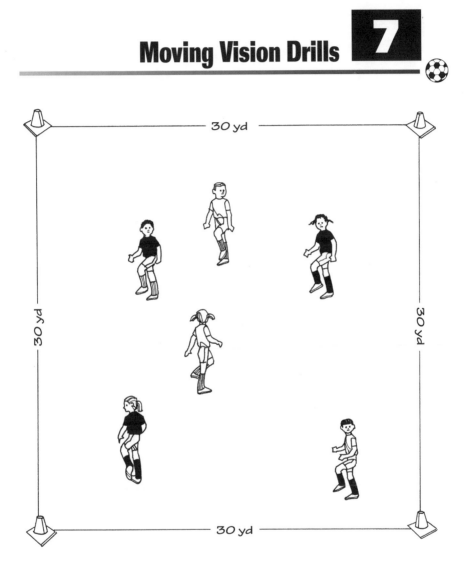

fore adding a ball. When a ball is added, vision is adversely affected. Beginning players, especially, like to look down at the ball
to keep it under control. Insist that they look left and right during
the sequence so that they break eye contact with the ball. If they
seem out of control, ask them to slow down.

Related Drills   5, 6

8 Volcano Drill

PURPOSE

To help develop an understanding of changing direction.

EQUIPMENT

Four game markers plus one game marker for each player

TIME

Five minutes

PROCEDURE

1. Position players in a scattered formation in a 20-yard-by-20-yard grid.
2. Within the grid, scatter approximately 16 markers, or one for each player. Players will pretend these markers are volcanoes (see figure).
3. On the coach's signal, players will move through the grid.
4. As the players approach a volcano, they must quickly change directions to avoid being burned by any lava.
5. Challenge the players to see how many volcanoes they can pass in 30 seconds.

KEY POINTS

This drill will help players begin to understand feinting. Coaches should demonstrate that to change directions quickly, players should flex one leg slightly and quickly push off the inside of the same foot. Encourage players to exaggerate this push-off in a lateral direction. By flexing the leg, players can apply more force in this lateral direction. Incorporate in this shifting of weight from one direction to another different body parts including the head, shoulders, and arms. Have players experiment with combinations

Volcano Drill   8

of feints, for example, feint right, left, then quickly back to the right.

Related Drills   9, 10

Zigzag Drill

PURPOSE

To help develop an understanding of changing directions.

EQUIPMENT

Markers—4 yellow, 12 green, 12 red

TIME

Five minutes

PROCEDURE

1. Make a 20-yard-by-20-yard grid using yellow markers to identify the corners.
2. Place green and red markers in three rows in random order, for example, green, red, green, red, red, green, green, red.
3. Be sure that each row has a different order.
4. Divide players equally behind the rows (see figure).
5. Players will move down each row negotiating the markers. If it is a green marker, they must make a feinting move to the right and continue to the next marker. If it is a red marker, they must feint to the left.
6. After players finish row one, they move to row two and then to row three. Row-three players move to row one.
7. Repeat several times.

KEY POINTS

This drill encourages players to develop feinting moves both left and right. Often, players want to feint only to their dominant side. Coaches should encourage players to exaggerate movement using quick bursts of energy in lateral directions.

Related Drills   8, 10

Zigzag Drill

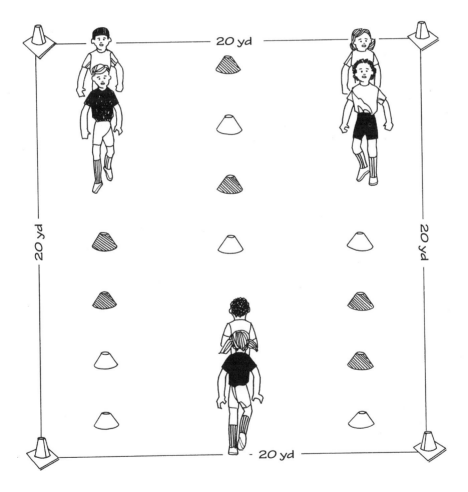

10 Sidewinder Drill

PURPOSE

To assess how well players are able to change direction and speed.

EQUIPMENT

Two game markers

TIME

30 seconds

PROCEDURE

1. Place two markers 10 feet apart.
2. On the coach's signal, players move laterally to touch one marker and then move in the opposite direction to touch the other marker (see figure).
3. Players repeat this action for 30 seconds.
4. Players count the number of times they touch the markers.

KEY POINTS

Use this simple drill to assess players' performance with lateral movement and change of direction and speed. You should not compare players' results. The purpose of this drill is not to determine which player performs the best, but simply to show players their individual improvement.

Related Drills   8, 9

Sidewinder Drill

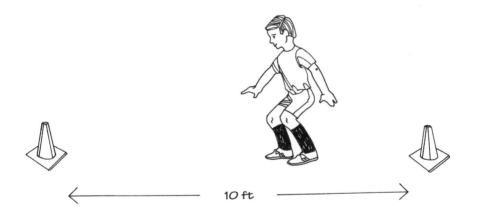

10 ft

11 Herky-Jerky Drill

PURPOSE

To demonstrate how change of speed can be used to create space.

EQUIPMENT

Four game markers for every two players

TIME

Five minutes

PROCEDURE

1. Place two players in a 10-yard-by-10-yard grid.
2. Have player B stand behind player A on the side of the grid (see figure).
3. Ask player A to move to the opposite side of the grid by jogging at a constant speed.
4. Request that player B follow player A, maintaining an arm's length distance.
5. Have player A move to the opposite side of the grid again, but this time by changing speeds—accelerating quickly, slowly, more slowly, more quickly—in a herky-jerky fashion.
6. Let players reverse roles several times during the five minutes.

KEY POINTS

Players should recognize that when they move at the same pace, the opponent can defend them easily, assuming both players are of equal athletic ability. In this drill, if a player moves at a constant pace, it should not be difficult to maintain an arm's length distance. However, if a player changes speeds quickly, defend-

Herky-Jerky Drill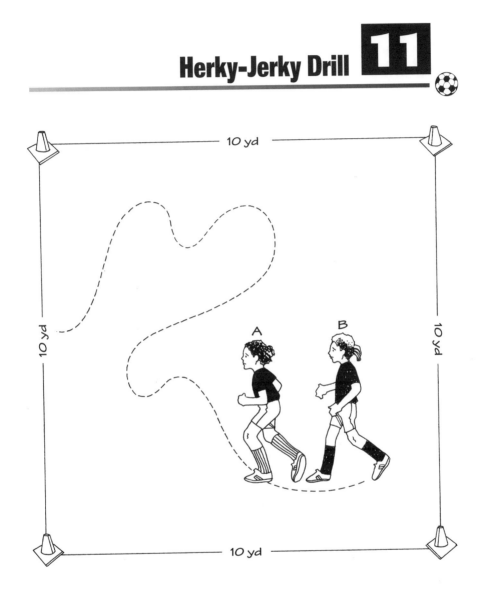

11

10 yd

10 yd

10 yd

10 yd

A

B

ing—or in this case maintaining an arm's length distance—becomes very difficult.

Related Drills   12, 13, 14

12 Copycat Drill

PURPOSE

To demonstrate how changing speed and direction can be used to create space.

EQUIPMENT

Four game markers

TIME

Five minutes

PROCEDURE

1. Two players stand side by side on a line of a 20-yard-by-20-yard grid (see figure).
2. On the coach's signal, player A begins to move, changing speeds in a forward direction.
3. Player B looks at player A and copies her movement.
4. If player A comes to a stop, she can reverse directions and go back, changing speeds toward the line where she started.
5. Player A may choose to change speeds and directions several times.
6. When the coach signals to stop, player B should still be beside player A.
7. Reverse roles several times during five minutes.

KEY POINTS

Coaches should encourage players to use short bursts of speed and change of direction to create space between themselves and their opponent.

Related Drills   11, 13

Copycat Drill

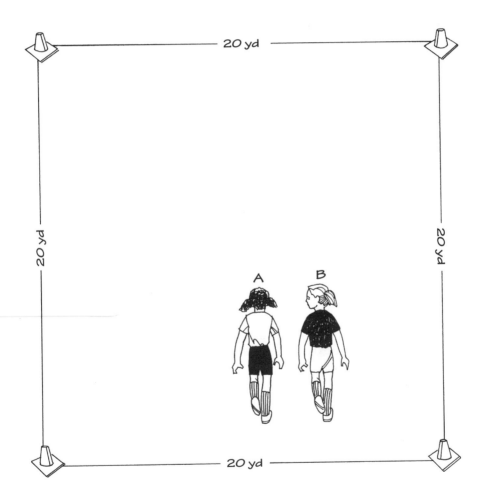

13 Monday Morning Traffic Drill

PURPOSE

To demonstrate how change of speed and direction can be used to create space.

EQUIPMENT

Four game markers

TIME

Five minutes

PROCEDURE

1. Scatter players with partners in a 15-yard-by-15-yard grid.
2. Player B will be the driver of the car. Player A is the backseat passenger who is being driven to work by player B (see figure).
3. Player B will be moving through the grid, changing speeds and directions and avoiding other drivers who are also on their way to work.
4. The backseat passengers are responsible for following their drivers closely, always maintaining an arm's length distance from them.
5. Reverse roles several times during the five minutes.

KEY POINTS

This drill can be equivalent to typical Monday morning traffic during rush hour, including traffic jams and fender benders. Coaches should encourage all players to be concerned with change of speed and direction, as well as the movement of the other couples to avoid collisions.

Related Drills   11, 12, 14

Monday Morning Traffic Drill

PURPOSE

To demonstrate how change of speed and direction can be used to create space.

EQUIPMENT

Four game markers for every two players, one flag belt for each player

TIME

Five minutes

PROCEDURE

Level 1

1. Position two players at opposite sides of a 10-yard-by-10-yard grid (see figure).
2. Players are wearing flag belts.
3. On the coach's signal, player A approaches player B and tries to pull one of her flags.
4. Player B tries to change speed and direction to get to the opposite side of the grid without having a flag pulled.
5. Player A will earn 1 point if she can grab the flag.
6. If player B can get to the opposite side of the grid, she earns 1 point.
7. The player who earns 5 points first is the winner.
8. Players then reverse roles.

Level 2

1. Place six players, two teams of three each, in a 20-yard-by-20-yard grid.
2. On the coach's signal, players try to steal the opposite team's flags.

Flag Tag Drill 14

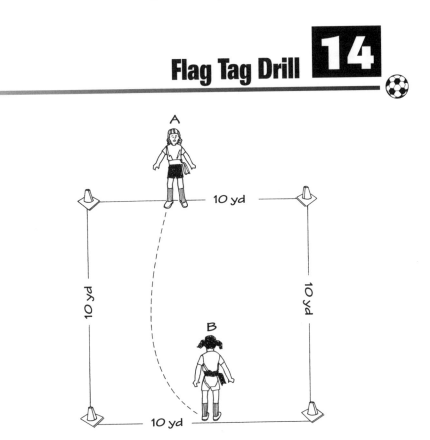

3. If a flag is pulled a player must wait to partner up with a teammate before helping to grab flags.

4. The team that captures all the other team's flags first is the winner.

KEY POINTS

Encourage player A to close the space toward player B by making a bending run at her and assuming a good defensive stance. A bending run means the defender will approach his opponent using a curved pathway instead of a straight line. A curved pathway allows the defender to guide the opponent toward a part of the square that reduces the amount of territory to defend. At level 2 spacing of players is important. Defenders should guide opponents toward a teammate or boundary lines using bending runs.

Related Drills   11, 12, 13

Exchange Drill

PURPOSE

To demonstrate how to change speeds and direction to avoid closed spaces.

EQUIPMENT

Four game markers

TIME

Five minutes

PROCEDURE

1. Position one player on each side of a 10-yard-by-10-yard grid (see figure).
2. On the coach's signal, players exchange places with the players on the opposite side of the grid by running in a straight line.

KEY POINTS

Four players moving in different directions at the same time could create a problem. Encourage players to change speeds to avoid moving into a closed space (another player). They must change direction with players opposite them to avoid these closed spaces.

Related Drill   16

Exchange Drill **15**

16 Team Exchange Drill

PURPOSE

To demonstrate how to change speeds and directions to avoid closed spaces.

EQUIPMENT

Four game markers

TIME

Five minutes

PROCEDURE

1. Divide players into four equal groups. Position one group on each side of a 10-yard-by-10-yard grid (see figure).
2. On the coach's signal, players exchange places with the group opposite them.
3. Vary the movement by walking, jogging, and running.

KEY POINTS

All players will be moving to get to the opposite side of the grid. Changing speeds with the adjacent group and changing direction with the opposite group will be essential to avoid closed spaces. This drill is more gamelike because it simulates the challenge of movement during games. Many times teammates and opponents will be clustered while moving in opposite directions toward each other. Other times, teammates and opponents will cross pathways with each other. Avoiding collision by changing speed and direction will reduce the possibility of injury.

Related Drill   15

Team Exchange Drill

10 yd

10 yd

10 yd

10 yd

Jackrabbit Drill

PURPOSE

To help develop balance while changing levels.

EQUIPMENT

Four game markers to identify grid plus one game marker per player for inside grid

TIME

10 minutes

PROCEDURE

1. Scatter game markers in a 20-yard-by-20-yard grid.
2. On the coach's signal, players move freely through the grid (see figure).
3. As they approach a marker, they jump with two feet as high as they can over the marker, landing lightly on two feet. As they land, they quickly change direction.
4. After repeating this action several times, have players jump, taking off with one foot and landing on both feet.
5. Then have players jump, taking off with two feet and landing on the left foot. Have them push off and change directions to the right.
6. Repeat this action and then switch, landing on the right foot and changing direction to the left.

KEY POINTS

Encourage players to use their arms to help generate force for jumping and for balance when landing.

Related Drills   None

Jackrabbit Drill

18 Shirt Tag

PURPOSE

To help develop an understanding of direction, speed, and level, and their relationship to movement.

EQUIPMENT

One scrimmage jersey for each player, four game markers

TIME

8 to 10 minutes

PROCEDURE

Level 1

1. Scatter players in a 20-yard-by-20-yard grid.
2. Each player should have a jersey tucked into the back of his pants (see figure).
3. On the coach's signal, players travel through space trying to grab the tucked scrimmage jersey of another player.
4. Have players try to grab as many shirts in a two-minute period as possible.
5. If a player has his jersey pulled, he must go outside the grid and do 10 touches on a ball before returning to the game. At the end of two minutes, stop and give all players a chance to get ready to start a new game.

Level 2

1. Repeat level 1 procedures 1 and 2.
2. Each player moves through grid with a ball while trying to collect jerseys.

Shirt Tag **18**

20 yd

20 yd

20 yd

20 yd

KEY POINTS

Encourage players to avoid closed spaces as they change directions, speeds, and levels. Change the specific skill that eliminated players must execute for each game, for example, 10 rollovers, 8 stepovers, and so forth. For variety, divide group into two teams and play team shirt tag. When playing shirt tag level 2, players who lose control of their ball while trying to collect a jersey must go outside the grid.

Related Drill   19

19 Number Tag

PURPOSE

To help develop an understanding of direction, speed, and level, and their relationship to movement.

EQUIPMENT

Four game markers

TIME

8 to 10 minutes

PROCEDURE

Level 1

1. Position all players on a line on one side of a 30-yard-by-30-yard grid.
2. Give each player a number from 1 to 4.
3. Have two players (defenders) stand between the line of players and the opposite line, which is safe territory (see figure).
4. Defenders call a number.
5. The player whose number they call tries to travel through open space to the safe line.
6. A player who is tagged must sit down.
7. When the next number is called, the player can try to free the players sitting down by touching them while on the way to the safe territory.
8. A player who is freed must try to get to the safe zone without being tagged.

Level 2

1. Repeat level 1 procedures, except players on the line must reach the safety zone while dribbling a ball.
2. If the ball is touched by a defender, the player must sit down.

Number Tag 19

Safe territory

30 yd

KEY POINTS

Coaches should encourage players to be in control as they change direction, speed, and level. Defenders should make bending runs as they try to capture players and avoid having two defenders chasing one player unless he is the only one left. During level 2 action, encourage numbered players to shield the ball from defenders while traveling toward the safety zone.

Related Drill   18

Dribbling Drills

Players who successfully demonstrate space and movement concepts are able to travel through space efficiently. Using these concepts when in possession of the ball, however, requires devoting time to improving ball skills. Players can do this in formal practice sessions and in informal sessions at home. The drills presented in this chapter will help to develop a portion of these ball skills—dribbling. Dribbling is the application of controlled touches on the ball with various surfaces of the foot so that the ball remains within playing distance of the dribbler. It is one of the ways to advance the ball through open space or to create open spaces when tightly defended. Players can dribble in a straight line using the inside or outside of the foot when moving through open space. Negotiating closed spaces requires changing position of the ball in relationship to the body and changing the position of the body in relationship to the ball (feinting).

Examples of changing the position of the ball in relationship to the body might include the following:

- **Pushaway**—using a surface of the foot to quickly move the ball away from the body and stop it
- **Pullback**—using a surface of the foot, usually the sole, to bring the ball back toward the body and stop it
- **Rollover**—using a surface of the foot on the ball to roll the ball forward, backward, or sideways

Examples of changing the position of the body might include the following dribbling moves:

- **Stepover**—stepping over the ball to its left with the right foot, pivoting back to right on right foot; may also be done with left foot going to right and pivoting back to left
- **Scissors**—stepping over the ball, feinting left, and touching ball to right with outside of right foot; may also be done with opposite feinting action
- **Walkover**—simply walking over the ball and turning

The dribbling drills in this chapter progress from least to most difficult. They include

1. stationary dribbling activities,
2. dribbling and movement with no defensive pressure,

3. dribbling with subtle pressure, and

4. dribbling with gamelike pressure.

Performing a skill from a stationary position is simpler than performing it while moving. When stationary, vision is not affected by negotiating space or other players. Therefore, a player can devote all of her visual attention to the skill, not to how and where to move. After players gain some confidence with dribbling skills from a stationary position, you will need to challenge them by placing them in motion. Do this without the added burden of defensive pressure. This will allow time and space for them to develop. As they become more competent with dribbling, add defensive pressure. This should be a gradual increase from subtle to gamelike pressure.

When using these drills, coaches should exercise patience and allow players to progress from a slow, methodical pace to a pace that is more gamelike. Expecting players to perform new moves under pressure before they are ready will lead to frustration and failure and may be responsible for their abandoning any effort to master new moves. Allow them to improve at their own rate.

Improved dribbling skills will enable players to maintain possession of the ball longer, create spaces for passing and shooting, and relieve defensive pressure.

20 Fancy-Footwork Drill

PURPOSE

To improve the ability to control the ball while in a stationary position with no defensive pressure.

EQUIPMENT

One soccer ball for each player, four game markers

TIME

10 to 15 minutes

PROCEDURE

1. Scatter players with a ball in a 20-yard-by-20-yard grid (see figure).
2. While stationary, players practice controlled touches on the ball.
3. Players can combine these touches in various ways to change speed, direction, or level. Encourage players to change the position of the ball in relationship to the body with pushaways, pullbacks, rollovers, and so forth.
4. Next, have players change body position in relationship to the ball with stepovers, scissors, walkovers, and so forth.

KEY POINTS

There should be time for hundreds of touches on the ball during each practice. Encourage players to explore ways to move the ball using the inside, outside, sole, and heel of each foot. Players may mirror individual moves demonstrated by coaches, but you should encourage them to create new combinations of moves. As they touch the ball, encourage them to maintain good vision constantly. For variety, and to reduce fatigue, use partners. Have one partner work on skills for a minute and then give the ball to the partner.

Fancy-Footwork Drill 20

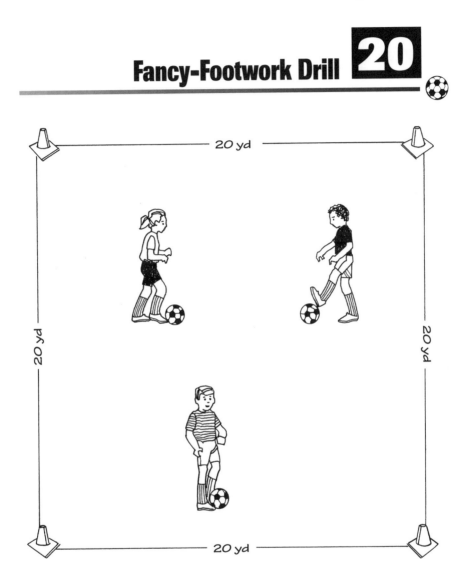

Repeat. Change formations using triangles, circles, and so forth to add variety to this drill. It is essential that you give players time to develop these skills from a stationary position without movement into other spaces and without defensive pressure. Players should practice these moves at home as part of a daily routine.

Related Drills   None

21 Follow the Leader

PURPOSE

To develop dribbling skills while negotiating space with no defensive pressure.

EQUIPMENT

One soccer ball for each player, four game markers

TIME

Five minutes

PROCEDURE

1. Divide group into lines of four or five players in a 20-yard-by-20-yard grid (see figure).
2. The first player in line is the leader and begins moving through the grid with the rest of the players following while dribbling their balls.
3. On the coach's signal, the last person in line will push his ball out approximately five yards in front of the leader, sprint after it, and become the new leader.
4. The new last person will repeat this action on the next whistle.

KEY POINTS

Coaches should encourage ball control by discussing force relationships of touching the ball with various parts of the foot and proper use of the general space provided so that the lines don't move into the same space. As players become more controlled in their movement coaches should allow players to do this drill without their signals.

Related Drills   22, 23, 24

Follow the Leader

22 Freedom Drill

PURPOSE

To develop dribbling skills while negotiating space with no defensive pressure.

EQUIPMENT

One soccer ball for every two players, five game markers

TIME

8 to 10 minutes

PROCEDURE

1. Space partners around a circle approximately 30 yards in diameter (see figure).
2. On the coach's whistle, the partner with the ball travels into the circle, practicing her individual moves as she encounters other players who are doing likewise.
3. After a minute of moving, the player with the ball returns and gives the ball to her partner, who repeats the action.
4. Players have complete freedom to use any of their individual moves during this drill.

KEY POINTS

Encourage players to use a variety of individual moves to change directions, speeds, and levels as they negotiate space. Refer to the demonstration on space and movement concepts if players are moving into closed spaces. This drill is the next step in the dribbling progression because it requires using individual moves to travel through space. The drill allows players the freedom to develop skills without defensive pressure.

Related Drills   21, 23, 24

Freedom Drill

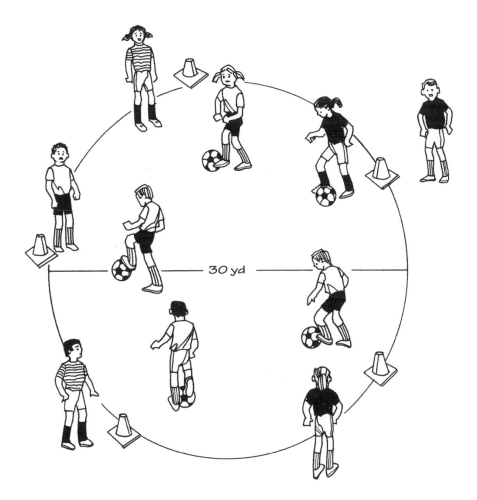

30 yd

23 Freeze Drill

PURPOSE

To develop dribbling skills while negotiating space with no defensive pressure.

EQUIPMENT

One soccer ball for each player, four game markers

TIME

7 to 10 minutes

PROCEDURE

1. Scatter players in a 20-yard-by-20-yard grid.
2. All players move freely with a ball through the grid (see figure).
3. When the coach signals by blowing a whistle, the players must freeze by bringing their balls to a complete stop.
4. Variations of this drill might include touching the ball with any body part on one side of the body, freezing on a specific number of body parts, or freezing at various levels.

KEY POINTS

This drill allows players to develop individual moves while negotiating space without defensive pressure. Encourage players to use body parts on their nondominant side. Freezing at various levels might include straight leg, crouched, or kneeling positions.

Related Drills   21, 22, 24

Freeze Drill

24 Partner Tag

PURPOSE

To develop dribbling skills while negotiating space with no defensive pressure.

EQUIPMENT

One soccer ball for every two players, four game markers

TIME

7 to 10 minutes

PROCEDURE

1. In a 20-yard-by-20-yard grid have each player choose a partner and hold hands.
2. One set of partners has a ball. The rest of the balls are outside the grid (see figure).
3. On the coach's signal, the pair with the ball acts as a chaser and moves through the grid dribbling the ball until they get close enough to another pair to pass the ball and hit them.
4. If a set of partners is hit with the ball, they must get a ball from outside the grid and become another pair of chasers.
5. The game continues until there is only one pair left.

KEY POINTS

This is a fun game that requires partners to coordinate their movements. Emphasize passing to hit other pairs and not shooting hard at them.

Related Drills   21, 22, 23

Partner Tag

25 Sprint Drill

PURPOSE

To develop dribbling skills and speed while negotiating space with no defensive pressure.

EQUIPMENT

One soccer ball for each player, four game markers

TIME

Five minutes

PROCEDURE

1. Scatter players in a 20-yard-by-20-yard grid with a ball.
2. The players travel through the grid until they hear the coach's whistle.
3. On that signal, players dribble their balls as fast as they can out of the grid (see figure).
4. They continue dribbling as fast as they can until they hear a second whistle.
5. Then the players dribble as fast as they can back to the grid, where they continue traveling through the grid at a moderate pace.

KEY POINTS

Present this drill only when players have developed sufficient ball control skills. Encourage them to push the ball away to open spaces at a distance of five to seven yards and then sprint to the ball. Kicking the ball as far as they can and sprinting after it is not the purpose of this drill.

Related Drill   28

Sprint Drill

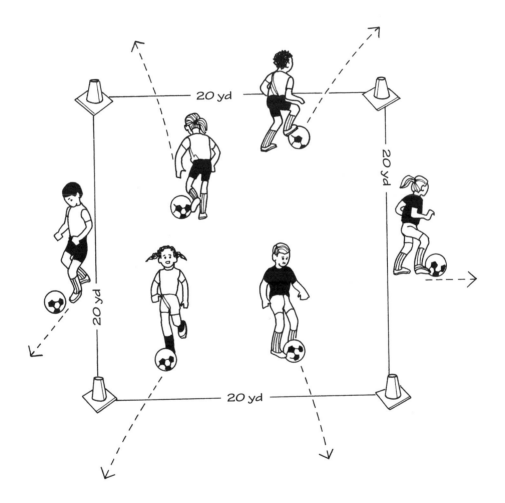

26 Circle Dribble Tag

PURPOSE

To help develop dribbling skills with subtle defensive pressure.

EQUIPMENT

Two soccer balls and four game markers for every six players

TIME

8 to 10 minutes

PROCEDURE

Level 1

1. Place six players in a 10-yard-by-10-yard grid.
2. Four players form a circle.
3. Two players, each with a ball, stand outside the circle on opposite sides (see figure).
4. Designate one of these players as the tagger.
5. On the coach's signal, the tagger has 30 seconds to catch the other player with a ball while both players are dribbling.
6. The tagger may cut through the circle, but the player being chased may not.

Level 2

1. Repeat level 1 procedures 1 through 6.
2. While the tagger is chasing the other player, teammates who have formed the circle move as a unit to shield the player being chased from the tagger.

Circle Dribble Tag **26**

KEY POINTS

Players need to use good visual habits to know when the tagger has changed directions. Changing directions and speeds frequently will help the player being chased.

Related Drills   None

27 Shake-and-Take Drill

PURPOSE

To develop dribbling skills used to create space and go to goal with defensive pressure.

EQUIPMENT

One soccer ball for each player, one marker for each goal, four goals

TIME

10 minutes

PROCEDURE

Level 1

1. Place a marker 40 yards from the goal.
2. A player dribbles toward the marker, executes an individual move to create space (a scissors move, for example), and then goes to the goal and shoots (see figure).

Level 2

1. Place two markers 40 yards from goal about 5 yards apart.
2. A defender stands on a line between the markers and tries to tackle the ball away from the attacker as he attempts to go between the markers to the goal.

Level 3

1. Player A stands 40 yards from the goal.
2. A defender stands 30 yards from the goal.
3. The ball is passed to player A.
4. When player A touches the ball the defender may pursue him.
5. Player A uses individual moves to create space to go to the goal.

Shake-and-Take Drill 27

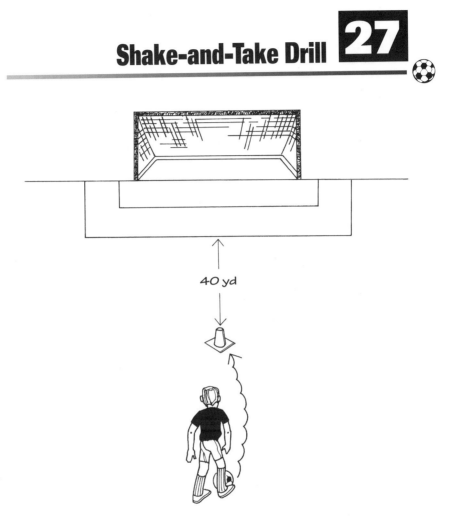

40 yd

KEY POINTS

Allow players to develop individual moves with imaginary pressure (the marker in level 1) until they experience success. When their skills have improved to the point where they need more challenge, add a defender who can move only laterally (level 2). This will add subtle pressure. A defender applies gamelike pressure at level 3. Do not rush players through their progressions. Use as many goals as are available, or make temporary goals, so players have many opportunities.

Related Drills   29, 30, 31

28 Sprint Challenge Drill

PURPOSE

To develop dribbling skills and speed when confronted with gamelike defensive pressure.

EQUIPMENT

One soccer ball for every three players, four goals

TIME

10 minutes

PROCEDURE

Level 1

1. Player A stands about five yards behind player B.
2. The coach passes the ball forward.
3. Player B must collect the ball, sprint toward the goal, and shoot before the defender can catch him.
4. Variations include serving balls at various speeds, directions, and levels.

Level 2

1. Repeat level 1 procedures 1 through 4.
2. Repeat the action but add a goalkeeper to increase the defensive pressure (see figure).

KEY POINTS

Encourage players to push the ball five to seven yards to maintain both speed and control. When adding a goalkeeper, restrict him by not allowing him to come off the goal line. As skills increase, add more goalkeeping pressure.

Related Drill   25

Sprint Challenge Drill

Coach

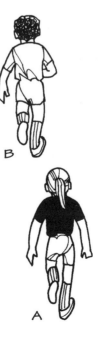

B

A

40 yd

29 Partner Dribble Game

PURPOSE

To help develop dribbling skills to create space with gamelike defensive pressure.

EQUIPMENT

One soccer ball and four game markers for every two players

TIME

8 to 10 minutes

PROCEDURE

1. In a 10-yard-by-10-yard grid, one partner stands on a line with a ball and the other partner stands on the opposite side of the square (see figure).
2. Player A passes the ball to player B.
3. When player B receives the ball, player A pursues her in an effort to close her space and touch the ball or force her out of the grid.
4. If player A touches the ball, she earns 1 point.
5. If player B can dribble safely to the opposite line, she earns 2 points.
6. The first player to earn 6 points is the winner.
7. Then they reverse roles.

KEY POINTS

The offensive player in this drill earns more points for being successful because this is an offensive drill. Encourage the offensive player to use a variety of moves to create space.

Related Drills   27, 30, 31

Partner Dribble Game **29**

10 yd

10 yd

10 yd

10 yd

A

B

30 Dribble Baseball Game

PURPOSE

To help develop dribbling skills to create space with gamelike defensive pressure.

EQUIPMENT

One soccer ball and eight game markers for every two players

TIME

10 to 12 minutes

PROCEDURE

1. Set up markers approximately 40 feet apart in the shape of a baseball diamond (see figure).
2. Player B passes the ball to player A, who is positioned at home base.
3. When player A touches the ball, player B can pursue her.
4. Player A can choose to dribble through any of the markers.
5. If she dribbles through the markers at first base, she receives 1 point; second base, 2 points; third base, 3 points.
6. If player A can go through any of the markers and return home before player B touches the ball, she earns 4 points for a home run.
7. Player B, the defender, can earn an out by touching the ball.
8. After three outs, the players switch roles.

KEY POINTS

Encourage players to use their individual moves creatively to change direction. If defenders are having difficulty getting outs,

Dribble Baseball Game **30**

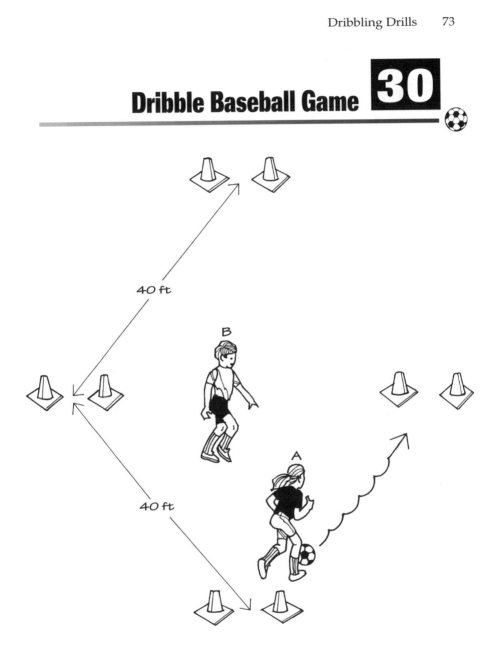

40 ft

40 ft

B

A

set a run limit. If players are having trouble scoring runs, widen the markers that form the bases.

Related Drills   27, 29, 31

31 One-Versus-One-for-All Drill

PURPOSE

To help develop dribbling skills to create space with gamelike defensive pressure.

EQUIPMENT

One soccer ball and two goals for every eight players

TIME

10 minutes

PROCEDURE

Level 1

1. Arrange eight players as shown in the figure.
2. Player A dribbles toward goal 1 in an attempt to score.
3. Player B defends.
4. After player A shoots, he becomes the defender and player B goes approximately 10 yards to the outside of the goal he defended.
5. Player C, who is waiting on the side of the goal that player B defended, becomes the new offensive player.
6. She receives a pass from the goalie and dribbles toward goal 2, which is approximately 30 yards away, while player A defends.
7. After player C shoots, she becomes the defender, and so on.
8. If the defender steals the ball at any time, he becomes the offensive player.
9. The defending player always goes to the side of the goal he defended.
10. Players rotate from offensive player, to defensive player, to the side of goal.

One-Versus-One-for-All Drill **31**

Level 2

1. Repeat level 1 procedures 1 through 10.
2. Add a goalkeeper.

KEY POINTS

This drill is very intensive. Limiting the number of players to eight will maximize the number of touches, yet allow for brief recovery periods. Present this drill initially with no goalkeepers to encourage scoring. As the players' skills improve, add a goalkeeper to increase the defensive pressure.

Related Drills   27, 29, 30

Passing and Collecting Drills

One of the most difficult tasks coaches have is developing their players' ability to connect consecutive passes. To accomplish this, players must develop efficient passing and collecting techniques. Collecting is the ability to gather in and control the ball using various body parts.

Besides developing passing and collecting techniques, players must learn to make good decisions about to whom to pass the ball. Players should make passing choices in this order:

1. Pass to a teammate who is in position to score.
2. Pass to penetrate the defense and advance the ball in a forward direction.
3. Pass to a teammate who can relieve defensive pressure so that the offensive team can retain possession of the ball.

Passing choices may be limited somewhat by a player's physical ability, skill level, position on the field, or even the quality of the opponent. Passing choices may be enhanced by movement of players off the ball, improved skill level, taking risks, and maintaining good field vision.

This chapter presents drills in a progression:

1. Stationary passes to stationary target
2. Stationary passes to moving target
3. Moving passes to stationary target
4. Moving passes to moving target
5. Passing skills with subtle pressure
6. Passing skills with gamelike pressure

The drills emphasize the development of short-passing techniques. Encourage young players to develop short-passing techniques that will allow them to deliver accurate, crisp, flat passes. Instruct players to rotate the heel of the kicking foot toward the target in a locked position to allow the large surface of the inside of the foot to contact the ball. The foot should contact the upper half of the ball, which will provide top spin on the ball and make it stay low (flat) to the ground. Encourage players to exaggerate their follow-through with a high knee lift of the kicking foot. In the first stage of this progression players learn how hard or softly they must kick a ball for it to travel a certain distance. Players will learn to judge leg speed and not kick the ball with the same force regardless of the situation.

The next stage of the passing progression requires a stationary player to pass to a stationary target. This develops proper passing techniques by excluding performance inhibitors such as motion and defensive pressure.

When players have improved their passing techniques, challenge them by adding motion. Begin with the player passing to a moving target. This will require players to understand the relationships among the speed of the target, the distance of the target, and the speed and angle of the pass. This scenario becomes more challenging in the next phase of the progression as you put the passers in motion. Now, they must compute all the things involved with passing to a moving target while negotiating space themselves. Many beginning players may find this a visual nightmare. To limit frustration, have players proceed slowly at first, gradually increasing their speed.

The final stage of the progression adds defensive pressure, which reduces time and space for decision making. Progress from subtle to gamelike defensive pressure according to the ability of the players.

As the players become more competent with passing skills, the quality of their play should improve. They should begin using soccer terminology that refers to the direction of the pass:

- **Through pass**—a pass that splits two defenders
- **Square pass**—a pass played to a player laterally (to the side)
- **Back pass**—a pass played in a backward direction, often referred to as a drop

With good communication and improved passing skills, your players' style of play will change from an individualistic, do-it-yourself type in which they always want to dribble, to one that is more team oriented and intentional in design.

PURPOSE

To help develop an understanding of the application of force when passing the ball.

EQUIPMENT

One soccer ball for every two players

TIME

Five to seven minutes

PROCEDURE

1. Players stand approximately five yards from the sideline (see figure).
2. Ask players to kick the ball so that it stops on the line.
3. Repeat several times.
4. Request players to repeat this action from 10-, 20-, and 30-yard distances.
5. Use partners to retrieve balls.

KEY POINTS

Discuss the proportional relationship between leg speed and distance the ball will travel. Encourage players to use proper kicking technique for making flat passes.

Related Drills   None

Force Challenge Drill **32**

Sideline

33 Partner Passing Drill

PURPOSE

To help develop passing accuracy and collection skills from a stationary passer to a stationary target with no defensive pressure.

EQUIPMENT

One soccer ball for every two players, four game markers

TIME

8 to 10 minutes

PROCEDURE

Level 1

1. Position players in a scattered formation in a 30-yard-by-30-yard grid.
2. Partners should be about 10 yards apart.
3. Players will pass to their partners, who will collect the ball and return the pass (see figure).
4. Encourage players to speak aloud the sequence of collect, look, look right, and pass.
5. Repeat looking left, or combining left and right, before returning the pass.

Level 2

1. Repeat level 1 procedures 1 through 5.
2. Vary this activity by using three players in a triangle or several players in a circle formation.
3. After a stationary player passes to a stationary target, she may run to that player's space.

Partner Passing Drill 33

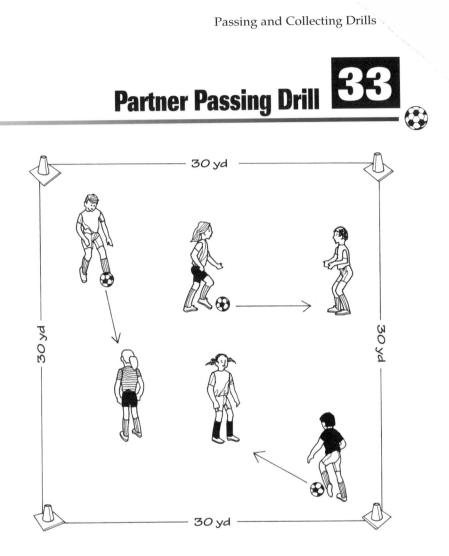

KEY POINTS

It is important for beginning players to stop the ball before returning it to their partner. Encourage players to relax the part of the body used for stopping the ball as this will have a cushioning effect. By stopping the ball, players will improve the accuracy of passes because it's easier to strike a stationary ball than one in motion. Level 2 incorporates movement after the pass. This will help to establish the philosophy that the passer should continue to be a player instead of becoming a spectator after passing. Later this movement will lead to executing wall passes.

Related Drills 34, 35

Thread-the-Needle Drill

PURPOSE

To help improve passing accuracy and collection skills from a stationary passer to a stationary target with no defensive pressure.

EQUIPMENT

One soccer ball and two game markers for every two players

TIME

Five minutes

PROCEDURE

1. Scatter partners with two cones between them (see figure).
2. Place cones initially about three or four yards apart.
3. Instruct players to pass to each other by having the ball go between the markers.
4. Have some fun with this drill by making it a game.
5. On the coach's signal players begin passing.
6. After each successful pass they take one step backward.
7. If the ball does not go between the markers, players must return to the starting point and begin again.
8. After two minutes stop and see how far apart partners are.

Thread-the-Needle Drill **34**

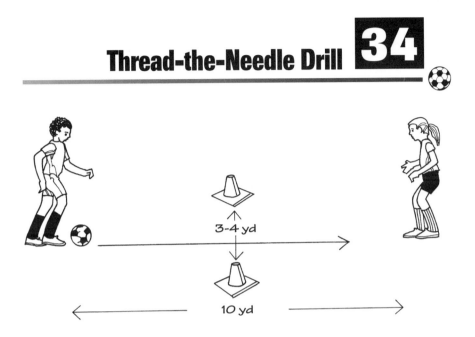

3-4 yd

10 yd

KEY POINTS

Begin this drill with partners approximately 10 yards apart. As the skill level of the players improves, increase the distance between the players and decrease the distance between the markers. To assess player performance, count how many times the players are able to pass the ball between the markers in 20 attempts. Insure that players are collecting and bringing the ball to a stop before returning the pass.

Related Drills   33, 35

35 Tunnel Connection Drill

PURPOSE

To help improve passing accuracy and collection skills from a stationary passer to a stationary target with no defensive pressure.

EQUIPMENT

One soccer ball for every three players

TIME

Five to seven minutes

PROCEDURE

1. Three players stand in a line approximately 10 yards apart (see figure).
2. Player A passes the ball through player B's legs to player C.
3. Player B then switches with player A.
4. Player C passes through player A's legs to player B and then switches with player A.
5. Repeat action several times.

KEY POINTS

Encourage players to collect and wait for their partners to get to their position before passing. Without patience, spacing becomes a problem with this drill. If necessary, place markers at 10-yard intervals to help players with spacing.

Related Drills   33, 34

Tunnel Connection Drill  **35**

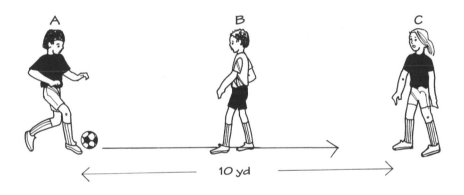

od-Bye Drill

PURPOSE

To help develop passing accuracy and collection skills from a stationary passer to a stationary target and initiate movement after the pass with no defensive pressure.

EQUIPMENT

One soccer ball and four game markers for every three players

TIME

Five to seven minutes

PROCEDURE

Level 1

1. Position three players in a 10-yard-by-10-yard grid so that they each occupy a corner of the grid (see figure).
2. Player A will pass to player B, then say good-bye, and travel to the unoccupied corner of the grid.
3. Player B then passes to player C, says good-bye, and travels to the corner vacated by player A.
4. Repeat this action several times.

Level 2

1. After players feel comfortable with the spacing provided by the 10-yard grid, remove the game markers.
2. Request that all players travel in threes, repeating the movement in general space.

KEY POINTS

Encourage players to deliver crisp, flat passes that will be easy to collect. Players should pass and move quickly to the open space.

Good-Bye Drill 36

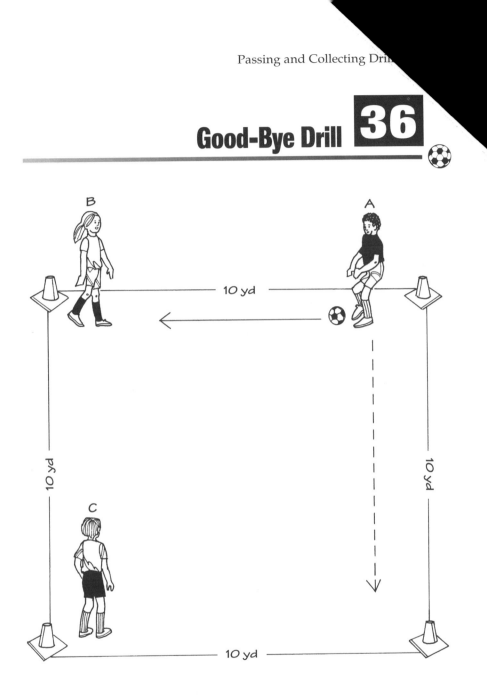

Reinforce this repeated action of pass and move in scrimmages and games. At level 2 encourage players to move through open spaces as they negotiate other players and maintain 10-yard spacing.

Related Drills   None

Circle Collection Drill

PURPOSE

To help develop passing accuracy and collection skills from stationary passer to moving target with no defensive pressure.

EQUIPMENT

Soccer balls for every player

TIME

10 minutes

PROCEDURE

1. Six players form a circle.
2. Each player has a ball (see figure).
3. Three players are in constant motion inside the circle.
4. As an inside player makes eye contact with a player on the circle, the ball is passed to her.
5. She returns the pass to the player who passed it and moves to another space to collect another pass.
6. Players forming the circle exchange places every one to two minutes.

KEY POINTS

Caution moving players inside the circle to pass through open spaces. Players on the inside should collect, look, and make a good decision concerning their next pass.

Related Drills   38, 39, 40

Circle Collection Drill 37

Hello Drill

PURPOSE

To help develop passing accuracy and collection skills from a stationary passer to a moving target with no defensive pressure.

EQUIPMENT

One soccer ball and four game markers for every three players

TIME

Five to seven minutes

PROCEDURE

Level 1

1. Position three players each in a corner of a 10-yard-by-10-yard grid (see figure).
2. Player C, closest to the unoccupied corner and not in possession of the ball, will move to the unoccupied corner and say the word "hello."
3. Player A, with the ball, passes to player C.
4. Player B then moves to the space vacated by player C to receive a pass from player C.

Level 2

1. As players become comfortable with spacing, remove game markers. Have several groups of players moving in one large grid repeating level 1 action.

KEY POINTS

Coaches should encourage players moving to space to give an oral reminder to the passer. In this drill they should be saying "hello." For the sake of consistency, coaches may want their play-

Hello Drill 38

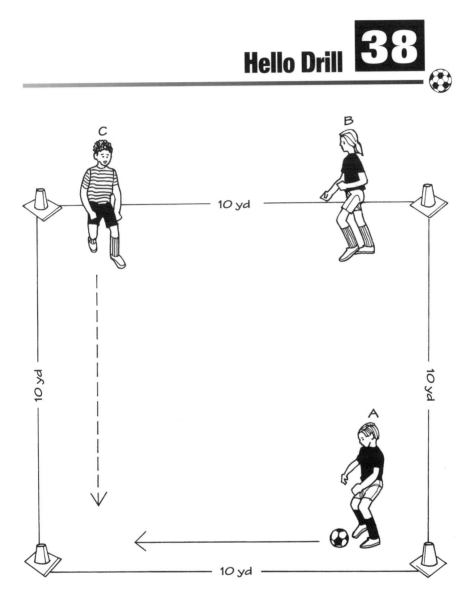

ers to say the word "space." Moving players should wait until the passer has controlled the ball and has made eye contact before initiating any movement. Discuss with players how delivering a soft pass to a player coming toward the ball will aid the collection process.

Related Drills   37, 39, 40

39 Spaceman Drill

PURPOSE

To help develop passing accuracy and collection skills from a stationary passer to a moving target with no defensive pressure.

EQUIPMENT

One soccer ball and three game markers for every two players

TIME

Five to seven minutes

PROCEDURE

Level 1

1. Position two players in a triangle identified by markers placed 10 yards apart.
2. Each player occupies a corner of the triangle (see figure).
3. The player without the ball runs to the unoccupied corner of the triangle and says loudly the word "space."
4. The player with the ball passes it to the moving player.
5. The player who passed the ball moves to the unoccupied corner to receive a return pass.
6. Repeat this action several times.

Level 2

1. Remove game markers. Have partners travel through general space using a triangular pattern with 10-yard spacing.

KEY POINTS

Encourage players moving to open space to make eye contact with the passer to insure that the passer has the ball in control to make

Spaceman Drill 39

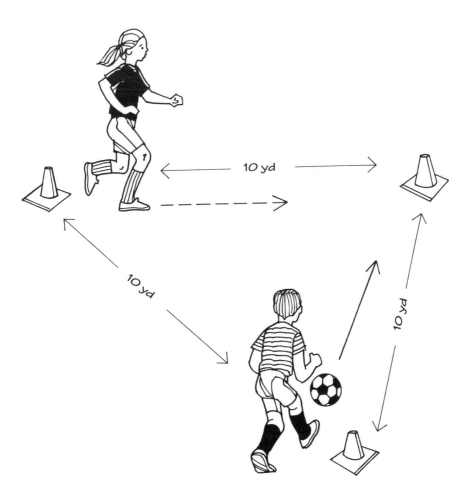

a pass. Instruct the passer to lead the player moving to space by passing the ball slightly ahead of him so he doesn't have to break stride to collect the ball. Timing runs and communicating well are important to the success of this drill.

Related Drills   37, 38, 40

Pendulum Drill

PURPOSE

To help develop passing accuracy and collection skills from a stationary passer to a moving target with no defensive pressure.

EQUIPMENT

Two soccer balls and four game markers for every three players

TIME

7 to 10 minutes

PROCEDURE

1. Position three players in a 10-yard-by-10-yard grid (see figure).
2. Two players will each have a ball on one side of the grid.
3. A third player will be on the opposite side.
4. The player without the ball will move to the unoccupied corner.
5. As she moves, the player on that side will pass the ball.
6. The moving player will collect the ball and return it to the player who passed it to her, and then run to the corner she just left to receive a pass from the other player.
7. Continue this back-and-forth movement.
8. After one minute, switch roles.
9. After skills improve, play the pendulum game by counting how many passes a player can make in one minute.

Pendulum Drill **40**

10 yd

10 yd

10 yd

10 yd

KEY POINTS

Encourage players to make flat passes with the correct amount of force that will be easy to collect. Discuss how the speed of the player will affect how far the passer must lead the pass.

Related Drills   37, 38, 39

PURPOSE

To help develop passing accuracy and collection skills from a moving player to a stationary target with no defensive pressure.

EQUIPMENT

One soccer ball and two game markers for every three players

TIME

Five minutes

PROCEDURE

1. Place two game markers three to four yards apart.
2. Position three players in a line (see figure).
3. Player B passes to player A, who collects, dribbles toward player C, and passes to player C.
4. Player C collects and dribbles toward player B, who took the place of player A.
5. Repeat this action several times.

KEY POINTS

This is a fast-paced drill that will provide lots of touches on the ball. Encourage players to make collection as easy as possible by delivering flat, soft passes.

Related Drills   37, 42, 43

Line Drill

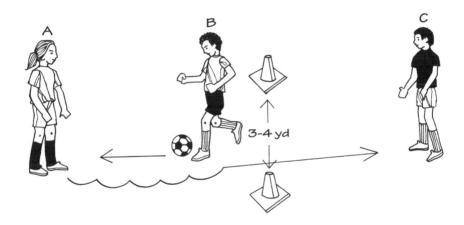

3-4 yd

42 Diagonal Passing Drill

PURPOSE

To develop passing accuracy and collection skills from a moving passer to a stationary target with no defensive pressure.

EQUIPMENT

One soccer ball and four game markers for every three players

TIME

Five minutes

PROCEDURE

Level 1

1. Position three players in a 10-yard-by-10-yard grid so that each occupies a corner space (see figure).
2. Player A dribbles to the unoccupied corner and passes diagonally to player B.
3. Player B dribbles to the corner vacated by player A and passes to player C.
4. Repeat action several times.

Level 2

1. Remove the game markers.
2. Have players move through general space repeating this action.

KEY POINTS

Players must use a controlled dribble to keep the ball in the grid. They must turn their nonkicking foot slightly toward the target before passing. This will allow the hips to rotate and the kicking

Diagonal Passing Drill 42

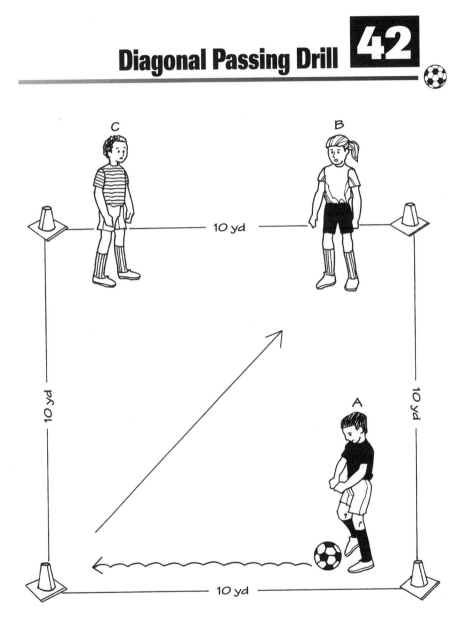

foot to swing outside of the ball before impact. At level 2 encourage players to maintain 10-yard spacing and avoid closed spaces.

Related Drills   37, 41, 43

43 Return-to-Sender Drill

PURPOSE

To help develop passing accuracy and collection skills from a moving passer to a stationary target with no defensive pressure.

EQUIPMENT

One soccer ball for every two players, four game markers, two sets of jerseys—one jersey for each player

TIME

7 to 10 minutes

PROCEDURE

1. Scatter players in a 30-yard-by-30-yard grid.
2. Divide the group with half the players wearing red jerseys, the other half green (see figure).
3. The green players, each with a ball, move freely in a grid.
4. As they approach a stationary red player, they will pass to her, collect the return pass, and then move through space finding another red team member to whom they will pass.
5. Repeat for one minute making as many passes as possible to different players.
6. Then reverse roles.
7. Vary this drill by delivering passes at different levels.

KEY POINTS

This drill will go more smoothly for beginning players if the stationary players collect the ball with their hands and then roll it to the passer, who should be moving to a new space. As the players

Return-to-Sender Drill 43

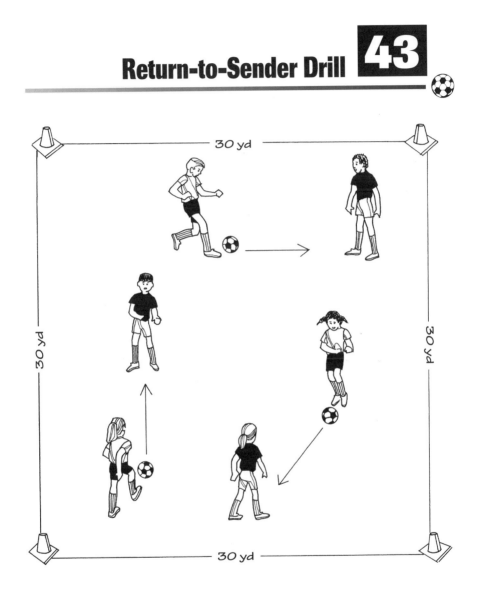

become more skillful, require them to collect with various body parts or execute one-touch passes.

Related Drills   37, 41, 42

Four-Corner Passing Drill

PURPOSE

To help develop passing accuracy and collection skills from a moving passer to a moving target with no defensive pressure.

EQUIPMENT

One soccer ball and four game markers for every five players

TIME

Five minutes

PROCEDURE

1. Position players in a 10-yard-by-10-yard grid so that players occupy the corners of the grid (see figure).

2. Player E will be outside the grid beside player A ready to occupy that space when player A leaves.

3. Player A moves toward, and passes to, player B, who begins to move when player A reaches the halfway point between them.

4. After passing to player B, player A continues to move and occupies player B's original space.

5. Player B collects on the move and passes to player C, who begins to move when player B reaches the halfway point between them.

6. Players continue this action of collecting while moving, passing to the next player, and then occupying his corner of the grid.

7. As passing skills improve, challenge players by counting how many times they can pass the ball around the entire grid in two minutes.

Four-Corner Passing Drill 44

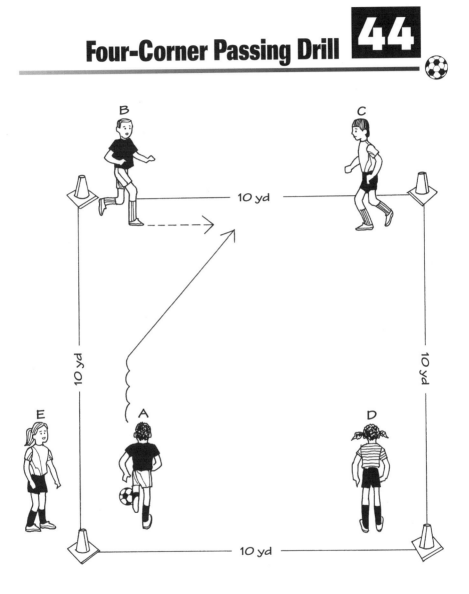

KEY POINTS

Passers should make eye contact with players they are passing to and should lead them with a pass that they can easily collect. You may use more players in this drill by positioning them by the corners outside the grid. As a player completes the pass, he would then go to the end of the line instead of standing by the marker.

Related Drills   45, 46

45 Pass-Dribble-Pass Drill

PURPOSE

To help develop passing accuracy and collection skills from a moving passer to a moving target with no defensive pressure.

EQUIPMENT

One soccer ball and four game markers for every two players

TIME

Five minutes

PROCEDURE

Level 1

1. Position two players in a 15-yard-by-15-yard grid (see figure).
2. Player A will pass to player B, who dribbles into open space and then turns and passes back to player A, who has moved to a new space behind her.
3. Repeat this action.

Level 2

1. Remove game markers.
2. Players repeat action moving in general space.

KEY POINTS

This drill requires players to pass the ball in a backward direction. Players taking space behind another player should communicate that they are in an open space by saying the word "drop." Players passing in a backward direction should begin developing the use of the heel to pass and changing the position of their body

Pass-Dribble-Pass Drill 45

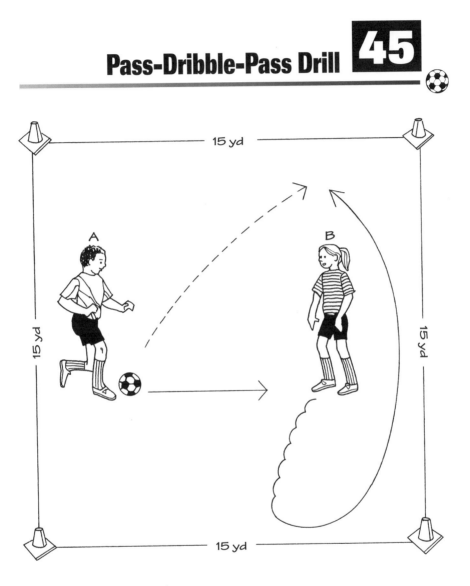

in relation to the ball as demonstrated on the stepover move. At level 2 encourage partners to communicate. With all partner groups moving in general space, partners sometimes become separated without this communication.

Related Drills   44, 46

46 First-Touch Drill

PURPOSE

To help develop passing accuracy from a moving passer to a moving target with no defensive pressure.

EQUIPMENT

One soccer ball for every two players and four game markers

TIME

Five to seven minutes

PROCEDURE

1. Scatter players in pairs in a 20-yard-by-20-yard grid.
2. Each set of partners has a ball (see figure).
3. On the coach's signal, the players begin to move through the grid.
4. The players with the ball pass to their partner, who must pass back on the first touch.
5. Partners continue moving using only one-touch passing.

KEY POINTS

Players must use good visual habits in negotiating space to avoid other players. Initially partners should move with spacing no more than three or four yards apart. As they become more proficient with their one-touch passing, they can separate by greater distances.

Related Drills   44, 45

First-Touch Drill

Invisible Man Drill

PURPOSE

To help develop passing and collection skills with subtle defensive pressure.

EQUIPMENT

One soccer ball and four game markers for every three players

TIME

Five to seven minutes

PROCEDURE

1. Position three players in a 10-yard-by-10-yard grid.
2. Players should be in a straight line with players B and C looking in the direction of player A (see figure).
3. Player B can move laterally, but not forward or backward.
4. Player C moves either right or left to receive a pass from player A.
5. Player B then faces player C, and players repeat the action.
6. After several chances, change defenders.

KEY POINTS

The addition of the defender will add subtle pressure to the passer because it will affect his vision. In fact, if player C does not move into open space, he is practically invisible to player A.

Related Drills   48, 49

Invisible Man Drill

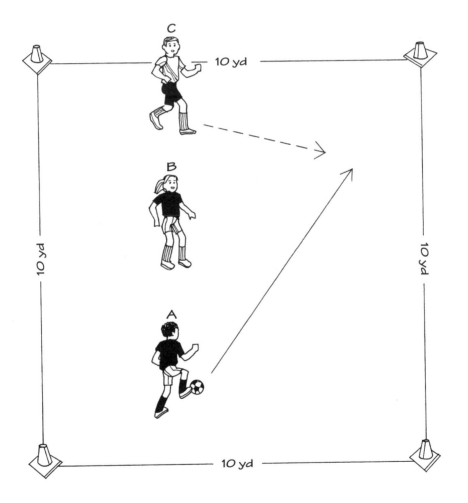

PURPOSE

To help develop passing and collection skills with subtle defensive pressure.

EQUIPMENT

One soccer ball for every six players

TIME

Five minutes

PROCEDURE

1. Position five players to form five points of a star (see figure).
2. Place one defender in the middle of the star.
3. Challenge players to make as many consecutive passes as possible without losing control or allowing the defender to touch the ball.
4. Do not allow players to pass the ball to players beside them.

KEY POINTS

This is a five-versus-one drill. The offensive players have a big advantage. Beginning players need this advantage to collect, look, and make good decisions with the ball.

Related Drills   47, 49

Star Drill 48

49 Monkey-in-the-Middle Drill

PURPOSE

To help develop passing and collection skills with subtle pressure, movement without the ball, and decision-making ability concerning the use of open versus closed space.

EQUIPMENT

One soccer ball and four game markers for every four players

TIME

10 minutes

PROCEDURE

1. Players occupy spaces by three of the markers.
2. A fourth player is in the middle and is affectionately referred to as the "monkey" (see figure).
3. The perimeter players are playing a three-versus-one keepaway game.
4. They are not allowed to pass the ball across the middle of the square.
5. This forces them to move constantly to support positions so the player with the ball always has two passing lanes from which to choose.
6. For example, if the ball is by cone A, players would support in spaces by cone B and cone D.
7. If the player in the middle, the defender, closes the space between A and B, then the pass is made to the player at cone D.
8. Then support positioning would go to cone A and cone C.
9. Since a player already occupies cone A, the player who was at cone B would move to cone C to support.
10. It is impossible for the defender to close both passing lanes.

Monkey-in-the-Middle Drill **49**

11. The defender earns his way out of the middle by touching the ball or forcing an error in passing or collecting.

KEY POINTS

Perimeter players must collect, look, and make a decision about passing choices. Perimeter players must communicate with each other concerning space. Variations might include limiting touches on the ball, using diagonal runs to space, or allowing dribbling to space.

Related Drills   47, 48

Cone Drill

PURPOSE

To help develop passing and collection skills with gamelike defensive pressure.

EQUIPMENT

One soccer ball and five game markers for every six players

TIME

8 to 10 minutes

PROCEDURE

1. Position a player on each side of a 15-yard-by-15-yard grid.
2. One player has a ball.
3. Place a game marker in the center of the grid.
4. Two players are inside the grid (see figure).
5. One is an offensive player; the other is a defensive player.
6. The offensive player must run around the cone and sprint toward the player with the ball.
7. The player with the ball passes to the offensive player if she is in an open space.
8. If the defender closes her space, the passer passes instead to another player on the grid.
9. The offensive player repeats going around the cone toward the new player with the ball.
10. The offensive player collects and returns the ball each time to the passer, who then passes to another player on the perimeter of the grid.

KEY POINTS

Challenge players to count how many times the offensive player receives a pass in one minute. Passers must give the offensive

Cone Drill **50**

players soft passes to collect. Defensive players work hard to close the space between the offensive player and the passer. Vary the degree of difficulty for collection by serving balls at various speeds and levels to challenge more advanced players.

Related Drills   51, 52

51 Check Out-Check In Drill

PURPOSE

To help develop passing and collection skills with gamelike defensive pressure.

EQUIPMENT

One soccer ball and four game markers for every six players

TIME

8 to 10 minutes

PROCEDURE

1. Position a player on each side of a 15-yard-by-15-yard grid.
2. One player has the ball.
3. Two players are inside the grid (see figure).
4. Player A runs away (checks out) from the ball, changes direction, and then sprints toward the ball (checks in) to receive a pass.
5. If the defender (player B) closes the space, the passer plays the ball to another player on the grid.
6. If the offensive player collects the pass, she should shield the ball for 5 to 10 seconds before returning a pass.
7. Challenge players to count how many consecutive passes the offensive player receives in one minute without the defensive player touching the ball.

KEY POINTS

Offensive players should move away from the ball at a moderate rate of speed. After changing directions, they should accelerate

Check Out-Check In Drill 51

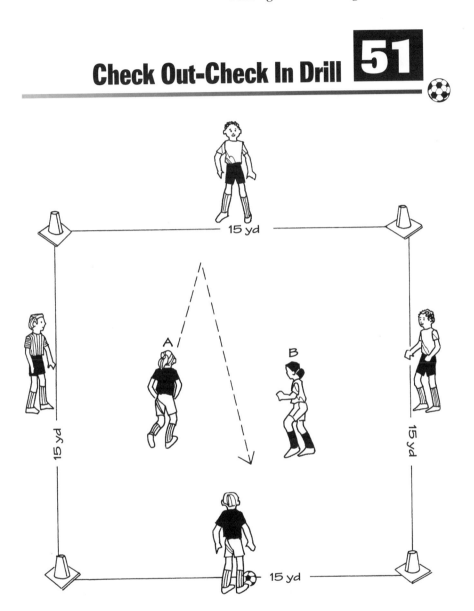

toward the ball. Changing speeds makes denying space more difficult for the defender.

Related Drills   50, 52

52 Beat-the-Clock Drill

PURPOSE

To help develop passing and collecting skills with gamelike defensive pressure.

EQUIPMENT

One soccer ball for every two players, four game markers, two sets of jerseys (one jersey for each player)

TIME

8 to 10 minutes

PROCEDURE

1. Divide the group into two equal teams with jerseys.
2. Position team A players, each with a ball, in a 30-yard-by-30-yard grid.
3. Members of team B are outside the grid.
4. On the coach's signal, players on team B enter the grid, try to gain possession of a ball, and kick it out of the grid (see figure).
5. After a team A player has his ball kicked out of the grid, he goes to a support position so that a teammate can pass him a ball.
6. The coach times how long it takes the defensive team to get all the balls out of the grid.
7. Then the teams switch roles.

KEY POINTS

Team A players should move to open space to maintain possession of the ball. Should they lose possession, they should move to

Beat-the-Clock Drill 52

a support position where they will try to collect, look, and make a good decision as to where to play the ball next.

Related Drills   50, 51

53 Never-Ending Three-Versus-Two Drill

PURPOSE

To help develop decision-making abilities concerning passing choices with gamelike defensive pressure.

EQUIPMENT

One soccer ball and two goals for every seven players

TIME

10 to 12 minutes

PROCEDURE

1. Place two goals approximately 30 yards apart.
2. Position players so that there are three offensive players in the middle of the field ready to score against two defenders (see figure).
3. Position two defenders at each end of the field.
4. On the coach's signal, the three offensive players pass the ball until they get close enough to the goal to shoot.
5. The player who takes the shot then joins the two defenders to try to score against the two defenders at the opposite end of the field.
6. If a defender steals a pass, that defending group goes on the attack with the person from whom they stole the pass.

KEY POINTS

There is a numbers advantage for the offensive players so there should always be an open player. Encourage players to make switching and overlapping runs to create space. Challenge players by allowing them no more than two touches on the ball.

Related Drills   None

Never-Ending Three-Versus-Two Drill

30 yd

54 One-Versus-One Drill

PURPOSE

To help develop decision-making abilities concerning passing choices with gamelike defensive pressure.

EQUIPMENT

One soccer ball, one jersey for defender, two jerseys (different color from defender jersey) for neutral players, and four game markers for every four players

TIME

8 to 10 minutes

PROCEDURE

Level 1

1. Position four players in a 15-yard-by-15-yard grid—one offensive, one defensive, and two neutral players (see figure).
2. The offensive player passes to one of the neutral players and then moves to open space to receive a return pass.
3. Players try to connect as many consecutive passes as possible.
4. If the defender gains possession, he becomes the offensive player.
5. After one minute of possession, switch roles.

Level 2

1. Use only one neutral player.
2. Apply a two-touch limit.

One-Versus-One Drill 54

KEY POINTS

Players must quickly change speeds and direction to create the spaces for passes. Variations of this drill include adding players to make two-versus-two or three-versus-three. Add goals to encourage finishing skills. Neutral players may not be defended.

Related Drills None

Heading Drills

Heading is a method of controlling the ball to pass or shoot. Like any other pass or shot, proper execution of this skill involves many concepts.

The intended direction or pathway of the ball will indicate what part of the ball the player should apply force to, what part of the head should apply the force, and how much force other body parts should generate. For example, if a player wanted to head the ball toward the ground, she would strike the ball with a downward motion of the forehead. If she wanted the ball to go upward, she could strike the bottom portion of the ball with the forehead. She can also use the top of the head to play the ball in a backward direction. If a player wants the ball to travel to the right, she has a choice of using the right side of her head or maneuvering her body before the ball arrives to strike it with her forehead. The opposite would apply for a ball that the player wants to play to the left.

The amount of force that a player should use on the ball is determined by how far the ball must travel after contact. A player generates force by bending at the waist and snapping the head and shoulders in a forward action.

The position of the ball to the player and the position of the player on the field are other factors that help determine proper heading techniques. Generally, players in the defensive third of the field want to head the ball high and wide away from their goal. Players in the midfield should be a little more precise as they are often trying to head balls to attacking players. Players in the offensive third of the field use heading skills mainly for scoring opportunities. Placement, not power, is essential for these players.

Most beginning players must overcome the fear of being struck in the face with the ball. When teaching heading skills, address this concern by using a sponge-type ball. In some cases it may be necessary to use a slightly larger and lighter ball similar to a beach ball to reduce fear. The teaching progression for heading should be as follows:

1. No defensive pressure, tossing softly to self from knees
2. Standing tossing to self
3. Standing with partner tossing
4. Heading with subtle pressure
5. Heading with gamelike pressure

Begin the heading progression by positioning players on their knees to insure proper balance of the lower body. Players thus can concentrate on the action of the upper body. As the players feel more comfortable with striking the ball with their heads, they should move to a standing position. This is the stage where players begin to learn about the contributions of the lower body to heading.

The next step in the progression has partners tossing while stationary and then while in motion. Emphasize positioning the body to get under the ball at this level. As players gain more confidence, have them jump and head the ball using a one-foot takeoff. Provide more challenging situations by offering heading drills with subtle and gamelike defensive pressure. Refining heading skills is another step toward adding more structure to the game and developing intentional play.

55 Toss-to-Self Heading Drill

PURPOSE

To help develop the skill of striking the ball with the part of the forehead known as the hairline, with no defensive pressure.

EQUIPMENT

One foam or beach ball for every player

TIME

Five to seven minutes

PROCEDURE

Level 1

1. Position players in a scattered formation.
2. Players should be on their knees, each with a ball. Players toss the ball slightly above their heads, strike it gently with their heads, and then catch the ball before it strikes the ground.
3. Repeat several times.

Level 2

1. After players have demonstrated correct heading techniques, have them then repeat this action from a standing position.

KEY POINTS

Visually demonstrate to players the location of the hairline. Emphasize moving the head to strike the ball instead of merely positioning the head so the ball will hit it. Insist that players strike the ball with their eyes open and mouths closed. This will prevent them from biting their tongues later when using a harder ball. At

Toss-to-Self Heading Drill

level 2 encourage players to establish a good base of support by slightly flexing their knees and positioning their feet a little more than shoulder-width apart.

Related Drills   56, 57

56 Partner Heading Drill

PURPOSE

To help develop proper heading technique with no defensive pressure.

EQUIPMENT

One foam, sponge, or beach ball for every two players, four game markers

TIME

Five minutes

PROCEDURE

Level 1

1. Position players in a 30-yard-by-30-yard grid with a partner.
2. Each set of players has a ball.
3. The player with the ball tosses to himself and heads the ball to his partner, who will catch, toss, and head it back.

Level 2

1. Instead of tossing to himself, the player tosses to his partner, who returns the ball by heading.
2. Players should be about five yards apart to begin this phase.
3. Gradually increase distance as both tossing and heading skills improve.

Level 3

1. The partner tosses to the player in motion, who returns the ball by heading.
2. The player in motion should vary directions forward, backward, left, and right.

Partner Heading Drill **56**

KEY POINTS

Partners should select a type of ball with which they feel comfortable. Emphasize bending at the waist in a backward direction and then thrusting forward to contact the ball to generate more force. Players should flex knees and extend arms to improve balance.

Related Drills   55, 57

57 Short and Long Heading Drill

PURPOSE

To help develop force relationships when heading with no defensive pressure.

EQUIPMENT

Two soccer balls and four game markers for every three players

TIME

Five to seven minutes

PROCEDURE

Level 1

1. Position three players in a 10-yard-by-10-yard grid.
2. Players B and C each have a ball (see figure).
3. Player B takes a position five yards from player A. Player B tosses to player A, who returns the ball by heading. Player C, who takes a position 10 yards from player A, then tosses, and player A repeats the heading action.

Level 2

1. After the first toss, only heading skills are allowed.
2. Player B tosses to player A.
3. Player A heads to player C.
4. Player C heads to player A, who returns the ball by heading to player B.
5. Repeat this action.

KEY POINTS

Players will need to generate different amounts of force because of the varying distances the ball must travel. Emphasize that the

Short and Long Heading Drill 57

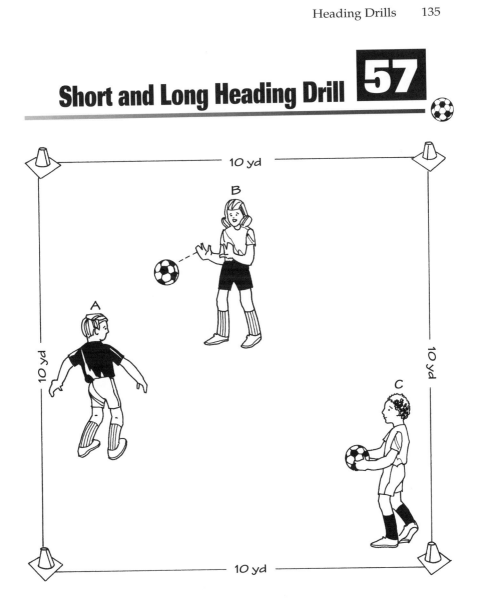

speed with which the head strikes the ball is the major factor in generating this force. Players can increase head speed by bending at the waist and thrusting the upper body forward. At level 2 use only one ball. Encourage players to move their feet to get good position for striking the ball.

Related Drills   55, 56

58 Star Heading Drill

PURPOSE

To help improve changing directions of the ball using heading skills with no defensive pressure at level 1 and with subtle defensive pressure at level 2.

EQUIPMENT

One soccer ball and one game marker for every five players

TIME

Five to seven minutes

PROCEDURE

Level 1

1. Position players in a star formation approximately 7 to 10 yards apart.
2. Place a game marker in the middle of the star (see figure).
3. The player with the ball calls another player's name, who must run around the marker and head the tossed ball to another player.
4. Continue this action.

Level 2

1. Repeat level 1 procedures 1 through 4.
2. Add a player in the middle of the star to provide subtle defensive pressure.

KEY POINTS

Encourage players to elevate before striking the ball. Insist that players head in forward, backward, left, and right directions. The

Star Heading Drill **58**

defensive player should be passive and not challenge in the air for the ball.

Related Drill   59

59 Three-Corner Heading Drill

PURPOSE

To help improve changing directions of the ball using heading skills with no defensive pressure at level 1 and subtle defensive pressure at level 2.

EQUIPMENT

One soccer ball and four game markers for every three players

TIME

Five to seven minutes

PROCEDURE

Level 1

1. Position three players on the corners of a 10-yard-by-10-yard grid (see figure).
2. Player A tosses the ball to player B.
3. Player B heads the ball to player C, who has moved to the open corner of the grid.
4. After player A tosses, she moves to the corner originally occupied by player C.
5. Player C tosses to player A, who heads the ball to moving player B.
6. Repeat several times.

Level 2

1. Repeat level 1 procedures 1 through 5.
2. Add defenders on the outside of the grid.

KEY POINTS

Emphasize to players that they should lead their teammates with head balls by placing the ball slightly in front of them, the same

Three-Corner Heading Drill **59**

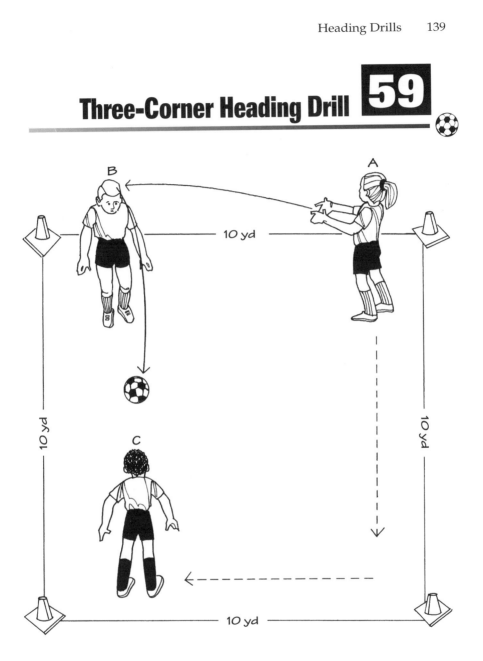

way as when passing with the feet. Adding defending players on the outside of the grid will encourage more preciseness with tosses and heading skills. Defenders are not allowed inside the grid and should subtly challenge in the air for head balls.

Related Drill   58

60 Jack-in-the-Box Drill

PURPOSE

To help improve heading skills with subtle defensive pressure.

EQUIPMENT

One soccer ball and two game markers for every three players

TIME

Five minutes

PROCEDURE

1. Position three players in a line.
2. Players A and C are approximately 10 yards apart, while player B occupies a position halfway between them (see figure).
3. Player A tosses over player B to player C, who will return the ball by heading.
4. Repeat several times and change roles.

KEY POINTS

Player B will provide subtle defensive pressure by obstructing the vision of player C. To add more defensive pressure, have player B jump as the ball is tossed. As the players' skills improve, reduce the distance between players B and C, and increase the distance between players A and C. Game markers will help provide proper spacing so players do not drift too far apart.

Related Drills   58, 59

Jack-in-the-Box Drill

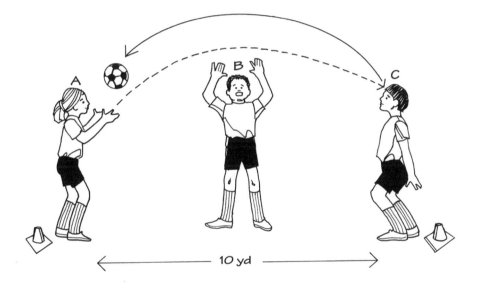

Show-for-Me Drill

PURPOSE

To help develop heading skills with gamelike defensive pressure.

EQUIPMENT

One soccer ball and four game markers for every three players

TIME

Five to seven minutes

PROCEDURE

1. Position three players in a 10-yard-by-10-yard grid (see figure).
2. Player B runs away from the ball, then quickly changes speed and direction, coming back toward the ball.
3. Player A tosses the ball for player B to return by heading.
4. Player C challenges player B for the tossed ball.

KEY POINTS

Player C must not take a ball-side position on the initial run by player B. Encourage player C to get to a ball-side position and make the first touch only after player B changes direction and moves toward the ball.

Related Drills   None

Show-for-Me Drill

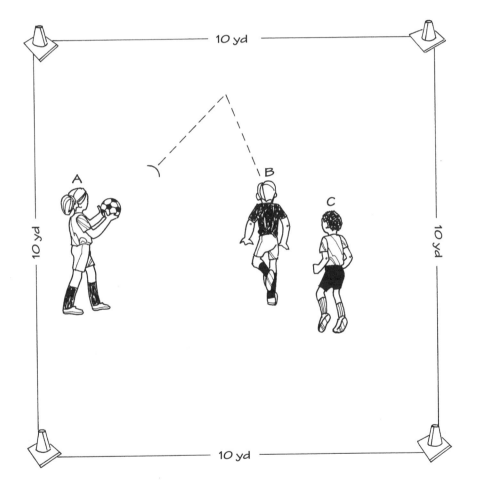

5.

Shooting Drills

Young players have the most fun when they are scoring goals. Therefore, practice sessions should include opportunities for lots of goal scoring. You can make these opportunities available during full-field scrimmages, small-sided games, and shooting drills. During full-field and small-sided games, vary procedures to encourage more goal scoring. Include games with no goalkeepers or restrict the movement of goalkeepers by having restraining lines. Adding more goals, or enlarging the ones being used, are other possibilities for increasing goal production.

Goal production will also improve as a result of an improvement in shooting skills. One of the ways to improve shooting skills is through drill work. Shooting drills can help develop the shooting skills necessary to be a successful goal scorer. Develop your players' shooting skills progressively. The drills in this chapter are designed to improve shooting skills using the following progression:

1. Stationary ball shot by a stationary player
2. Stationary ball shot by a moving player
3. Moving ball shot by a stationary player
4. Moving ball shot by a moving player
5. Creating shooting opportunities with subtle, then gamelike, defensive pressure

Beginning players need to understand how to strike the ball properly when shooting. Players can often take shots from close range with the inside of the foot, much like a pass. Using the inside of the foot will enhance shooting accuracy. When more power is necessary, emphasize striking the ball with the instep of the foot with the toes pointed downward and the ankle locked. Placement of the nonkicking foot will affect the elevation of the shot. To insure that the shot stays low, players should place the nonkicking foot slightly ahead of the ball. To focus your players' shooting attention on striking the ball, eliminate distracting elements such as motion of the ball, motion of the shooter, or defenders. Do this by beginning the shooting progression with a stationary ball and a stationary shooter.

As shooting techniques improve, slowly increase the challenge by putting the shooter in motion before striking the ball. This motion will initially distract from the preciseness of striking techniques because the player's vision must serve a dual purpose. The player's vision must help both to negotiate space getting to the ball and to place the foot on the ball at the correct location.

As players become more confident, increase the challenge by placing the shooter and ball in motion. This is certainly more gamelike. Make this transition less difficult for players by serving them balls at moderate speed that are not bouncing. As they become more competent, serve them balls at various speeds and levels.

The final step in the progression requires adding defensive pressure. Begin with subtle pressure and graduate to more gamelike pressure. Keep these drills fast paced and avoid having players stand in lines by using all the goals available and many balls. If necessary, create temporary goals. You may want to incorporate shooting drills as part of a circuit where some team members practice shooting, while others practice fast footwork skills, passing, and so forth.

62 Partner Stationary Shooting Drill

PURPOSE

To help develop proper kicking techniques for shooting a stationary ball from a stationary position with no defensive pressure.

EQUIPMENT

One soccer ball for every two players

TIME

7 to 10 minutes

PROCEDURE

1. In a scattered formation, position partners so that they are 10 to 15 yards apart.
2. The partner without the ball should assume a goalkeeper's stance, with hands in a ready position.
3. The other partner will approach the stationary ball and shoot, trying to hit his partner.

KEY POINTS

Beginning players are sometimes not accurate while shooting. To allow for this, it may be necessary to increase the number of goalkeepers a player is shooting toward. For example, space three goalkeepers in ready positions about 10 feet apart and have the shooter aim for the middle one. Players will spend less time chasing errant kicks. Reinforce a philosophy of accuracy over power during this drill. To help improve accuracy, encourage players to watch their foot strike the ball. Emphasize the use of the instep position of the foot as opposed to the toes.

Related Drills   63, 64

Partner Stationary Shooting Drill **62**

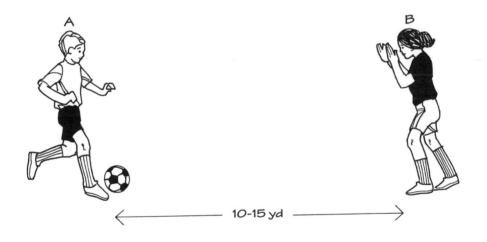

PURPOSE

To help develop proper kicking techniques for shooting a stationary ball from a stationary position with no defensive pressure.

EQUIPMENT

One soccer ball for every three players

TIME

7 to 10 minutes

PROCEDURE

1. Position three players in a line approximately 10 yards apart (see figure).
2. Player A shoots the ball at player B, who is in a goalkeeper's stance.
3. Player B collects the ball and rolls it to player C.
4. Player C stops the ball and then shoots at player B.
5. After several shots, rotate players.

KEY POINTS

Emphasize striking a stationary ball with the instep of the foot. Promote the philosophy of shooting accuracy over shooting power. As the players become more competent with shooting skills, increase the distance between players.

Related Drills   62, 64

Three-Player Shooting Drill

A

B

C

64 Open-Corner Drill

PURPOSE

To help develop shooting accuracy from a stationary position with a stationary ball and no defensive pressure.

EQUIPMENT

One soccer ball per player, four goals

TIME

10 to 12 minutes

PROCEDURE

Level 1

1. Place several balls in a row approximately 12 to 15 yards from the goal (see figure).
2. Players will shoot the balls into the unoccupied goal.

Level 2

1. Repeat level 1 procedures 1 and 2.
2. Place a goalkeeper slightly to one side of the goal.
3. Challenge the players to shoot to the unoccupied corner.

KEY POINTS

Once players have developed a proper kicking technique, they should develop an understanding of placement. Encourage players, during level 1 of this drill, to shoot for the corners. When you add a goalkeeper at level 2, restrict the keeper's movement by using game markers to establish how far she may move on the goal line. Do this drill as part of small-group work using portable

Open-Corner Drill **64**

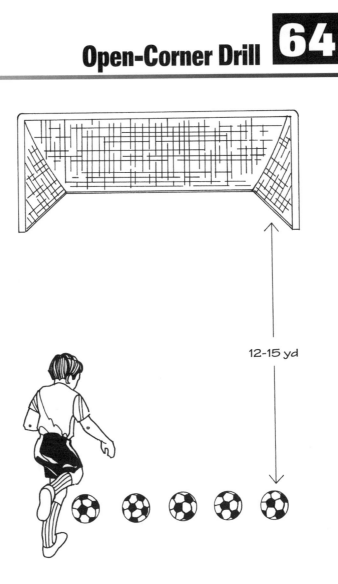

12-15 yd

or temporary goals, or as part of station work as players are arriving to practice. Using the drill in large-group work will result in too much standing.

Related Drills   62, 63

65 Run-and-Shoot Drill

PURPOSE

To help develop proper kicking technique when the shooter is in motion, the ball is stationary, and there is no defensive pressure.

EQUIPMENT

Four soccer balls, one goal, four game markers for every four players

TIME

10 to 12 minutes

PROCEDURE

Level 1

1. Place several balls in a row in a 15-yard-by-15-yard grid.
2. The shooter runs around one of the markers and shoots the ball in the goal.
3. Repeat several times with the shooter running around a different marker each time.

Level 2

1. Repeat level 1 procedures 1 and 2.
2. Place a goalkeeper outside each goal post.
3. As the shooter makes the turn around the marker, signal one of the goalkeepers to step in one corner of the goal.
4. The shooter must shoot to the unoccupied corner.

KEY POINTS

Requiring the shooter to run around different markers will vary the angle of the kick. During level 2 action, goalkeepers must stay inside the goal on their side. This means shooters must look up to determine where to place the ball. During level 1, one player

Run-and-Shoot Drill 65

shoots, two retrieve balls, and one player resets balls for next shooter. During level 2, one player shoots, two act as goalkeepers, and the other retrieves balls. Coaches may want to use this drill as a station for circuit training. If you use this drill as a large-group activity, use regular and temporary goals. Emphasize shooting low at the temporary goals and high at the regular goals.

Related Drills   None

PURPOSE

To help develop proper kicking technique for shooting a moving ball by a stationary player with no defensive pressure.

EQUIPMENT

Six soccer balls and two goals for every five players

TIME

12 to 15 minutes

PROCEDURE

1. Position two goals approximately 30 yards apart.
2. Place two players, D and B, on the sides with several balls.
3. Player C is the shooter (see figure).
4. When player B serves the ball, player C shoots at goalkeeper A.
5. When player D serves the ball, player C reverses and shoots at goalkeeper E.
6. After six shots everyone rotates.

KEY POINTS

This drill is more gamelike and highlights the role of target players. By putting the ball in motion, the shooter's time for decision making is reduced. Emphasize that shooters must not only visually track the pathway of their foot striking the ball but also compute the speed, direction, and level at which the ball is traveling. To make this less complicated for beginning players, serve them balls that are flat and moderately paced. As skills improve, serve balls at various speeds and levels.

Related Drills   67, 68

Reverse Serving Shooting Drill 66

A

D   C   B

30 yd

E

67 Pass-and-Shoot Drill

PURPOSE

To help develop proper kicking technique by a stationary player shooting a moving ball with no defensive pressure.

EQUIPMENT

One soccer ball and two goals for every four players

TIME

12 to 15 minutes

PROCEDURE

1. Place two goals 30 yards apart.
2. Position players as shown (see figure).
3. Player B serves to player C, who shoots at goalkeeper D.
4. Goalkeeper D passes to player C. Player C passes to player B, who shoots at goalkeeper A.
5. Repeat several times and reverse roles.

KEY POINTS

Keep several balls in the goals for goalkeepers to pass. This will keep the drill fast paced. Encourage one-touch shooting to the corners of the goals.

Related Drills   66, 68

Pass-and-Shoot Drill 67

68 Over-the-Goal Shooting Drill

PURPOSE

To help develop proper kicking technique for shooting a moving ball at various levels by a stationary player with no defensive pressure.

EQUIPMENT

Three soccer balls and one goal for every three players

TIME

8 to 10 minutes

PROCEDURE

1. Position three players by placing one behind, one in front, and one in the goal (see figure).
2. Player A serves the ball over the goal to player C, who is approximately 15 to 20 yards from goal.
3. Player C shoots at goalkeeper B.
4. Player A will serve three balls; then players change roles.

KEY POINTS

Moving balls served at various levels are very challenging for beginning players. Allow the shooter at least one touch to settle the ball a little before shooting. As skills improve, request that the players shoot the ball toward the goal on the first touch. Emphasize striking the middle or top half of the ball on its descent. This will help to keep the shot low.

Related Drills   66, 67

Over-the-Goal Shooting Drill **68**

69 Alternating Shooting Drill

PURPOSE

To help develop proper kicking technique for shooting a moving ball by a moving player with no defensive pressure.

EQUIPMENT

Four soccer balls and one set of goals for every four players

TIME

8 to 10 minutes

PROCEDURE

1. Place two goals 30 yards apart.
2. Position two players in the center of the field (see figure).
3. Player B will serve balls alternately right and left.
4. Player A must go after the ball and shoot at the goal that is in the direction the ball is traveling.
5. Player A then returns to shoot in the opposite direction.

KEY POINTS

Moving players shooting moving balls must gather a lot of information in a short time. They must compute the direction, speed, and level of the ball; their speed; their angle to the ball; their level relative to the ball; the distance from goal; and the position of the goalkeeper. This is why the moving-ball–moving-player phase should be last in the shooting progression.

Related Drill 70

Alternating Shooting Drill 69

30 yd

70 Spin-Turn Shooting Drill

PURPOSE

To help develop creating space for shooting a moving ball by a moving player with no defensive pressure.

EQUIPMENT

One soccer ball and one goal for every two players

TIME

8 to 10 minutes

PROCEDURE

1. Position players in the offensive third of the field.
2. Player A, in the penalty box, makes a horizontal run and then checks back for the ball.
3. Player B will pass to player A, who returns the ball to player B with a one-touch pass.
4. After returning the pass, player A spins to the outside to create space for player B to return pass for a shot.

KEY POINTS

Players should pivot on the inside foot (the foot closest to the goal) when spinning to the outside. Players should alternate between spinning wide, to create enough space for a pass, and spinning close to the defender to get behind him.

Related Drills   None

Spin-Turn Shooting Drill 70

71 Four-Grid Pin Dodge

PURPOSE

To help develop shooting accuracy with no defensive pressure.

EQUIPMENT

Four soccer balls, nine game markers, 20 bowling pins

TIME

10 to 12 minutes

PROCEDURE

1. Divide the general space into four grids, each approximately 15 yards by 15 yards.
2. Place five bowling pins in each grid.
3. Divide players into four teams and position them on the outside of their grid with a ball (see figure).
4. On the coach's signal, players try to shoot and knock down the pins in the other grids.
5. If all of a team's pins are knocked down, they may continue to shoot at the pins in the other grids.
6. The last team to have pins standing is the winner.
7. Players may not enter their grids except for one member of the team who is the designated ball retriever.
8. The retriever's role is to clear the team's grid of any ball stopped there and pass it to a teammate.
9. Retrievers are not allowed to shoot while in the grid.

KEY POINTS

Encourage players to use a variety of shooting techniques by striking stationary and moving balls. They may chip the ball over their

Four-Grid Pin Dodge **71**

pins to shoot or they may dribble along their grid sidelines to get in position before shooting.

Related Drill   72

72 Arcade Shooting Drill

PURPOSE

To help develop shooting accuracy with no defensive pressure.

EQUIPMENT

One soccer ball, four game markers, 10 half-cone disks for every four players

TIME

8 to 10 minutes

PROCEDURE

1. Place five half-cone disks in a 15-yard-by-15-yard grid.
2. Place five more half-cone disks upside down on top of the original half-cone disks (see figure).
3. Position a player on each of the grid's four sides.
4. One of the players has a ball.
5. On the coach's signal, the player with the ball shoots at one of the disks to try to knock it off the other disk.
6. Another player from the grid shoots next.
7. Players rotate turns until all the disks have been hit.
8. Use several grids for a team.
9. Make a game out of this drill by seeing which group of players can first knock down the disks in their grid.

KEY POINTS

Emphasize shooting accuracy over shooting power. Players may choose to shoot balls that are stationary or in motion.

Related Drill   71

Arcade Shooting Drill 72

15 yd

15 yd

15 yd

15 yd

PURPOSE

To help develop shooting accuracy with subtle defensive pressure.

EQUIPMENT

One soccer ball, four game markers, one bowling pin for every six players

TIME

8 to 10 minutes

PROCEDURE

1. Position five players to form a circle.
2. Inside the circle, place four game markers to form a square.
3. Place a bowling pin inside the square (see figure).
4. Designate a sixth player to defend the pin without going inside the square.
5. Players will pass the ball until a good shot opportunity is available.
6. If a player shoots and knocks down the pin, she replaces the defender.

KEY POINTS

Emphasize to players that they should pass the ball quickly to make the defender change directions, thus creating space for a good shot.

Related Drills   None

Circle Pin Dodge

Three-Versus-One Shooting Drill

PURPOSE

To help develop proper kicking techniques for shooting a moving ball by a moving player with subtle defensive pressure.

EQUIPMENT

One soccer ball and one goal for every four players, one jersey for every goalkeeper

TIME

10 to 12 minutes

PROCEDURE

Level 1

1. Position players approximately 30 yards from the goal (see figure).
2. Offensive players A, B, and C connect a series of passes until one of them takes a shot.
3. One defender provides subtle pressure.

Level 2

1. Repeat level 1 procedures 1 and 2.
2. Add a goalkeeper to provide more defensive pressure.

KEY POINTS

Each offensive player must touch the ball before a shot may be taken. Encourage creative movement like switching and overlapping runs. To encourage goal scoring, give the offensive players a numbers advantage such as this drill provides.

Related Drills   None

Three-Versus-One Shooting Drill

Cat-and-Mouse Shooting Drill

PURPOSE

To help develop abilities to create space for shooting with subtle defensive pressure.

EQUIPMENT

One soccer ball and one goal for every two players

TIME

8 to 10 minutes

PROCEDURE

1. Position players as shown in the figure.
2. Player A passes to player B.
3. Player A then makes a bending run to offer passive defense against player B's penetrating moves.
4. Player B will collect and complete one or more individual moves to create space for a shot.

KEY POINTS

Player A must wait for player B to collect the ball before making his bending run. Emphasize subtle pressure by the defender since this is an offensive drill. Encourage a variety of individual moves by offensive players. To allow more scoring, do not initially use a goalkeeper. Use as many goals as possible.

Related Drill   76

Cat-and-Mouse Shooting Drill

76 Come-and-Get-Me Shooting Drill

PURPOSE

To help develop abilities to create space for shooting with subtle defensive pressure.

EQUIPMENT

One soccer ball and one goal for every three players

TIME

8 to 10 minutes

PROCEDURE

1. Position players in the offensive third of the field.
2. Player A will run away from the ball, then check back toward it and receive a pass from player B.
3. When player B touches the ball, player C runs to defend player A.
4. Player A must create space using individual moves to shoot.
5. Player C will be passive in playing defense.

KEY POINTS

Initially, space the server and the defender far enough apart so the offensive player has a distinct advantage. As the players' skills improve, move the defender closer to reduce the time the attacker has to shoot.

Related Drill   75

Come-and-Get-Me Shooting Drill

76

Wall Pass Shooting Drill

PURPOSE

To help develop abilities to create space for shooting with gamelike defensive pressure.

EQUIPMENT

One soccer ball and one goal for every four players

TIME

8 to 10 minutes

PROCEDURE

Level 1

1. Position players in the defensive third of the field.
2. Player A is the offensive player; player B is the defender.
3. Player A must pass to player 1 or player 2, as a target, then move to open space for a return pass and shot.
4. Player B should defend aggressively.

Level 2

1. The ball is served to player A.
2. Player A must collect and take on the defender with individual moves to create space for a shot or use players 1 and 2 for wall passes.

Level 3

1. Repeat level 2 procedures 1 and 2.
2. Add a goalkeeper to increase defensive pressure.

Wall Pass Shooting Drill 77

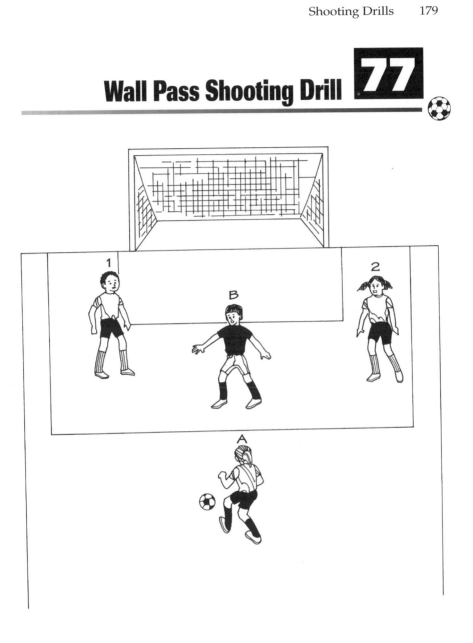

KEY POINTS

Encourage players to change speeds, using quick bursts to create spaces for shots.

Related Drills   None

6.

Game Progressions

The progression in player development in games should focus first on skill acquisition and movement concepts. You should initially limit the number of players in a game so that more time and space exist for decision making. As the players become more skilled and their knowledge base increases, the game progression will require the addition of more players, more rules, larger fields, and more team strategies. Detrimental to this process are emphasizing competition too early, confusing players with soccer terminology prematurely, and implementing rules and structure that are burdensome. It would be impossible to discuss all the changes that occur at each level concerning strategies, concepts, and so forth. Instead, I will discuss some of the major concerns and recommend this progression: 3-versus-3, 3-versus-3 plus goalkeeper, 7-versus-7, and 11-versus-11.

Three-Versus-Three

The three-versus-three, small-sided game is used for beginning players ages five to seven. Play this game on a field approximately 50 yards long by 30 yards wide. Goal size should be somewhere in the range of eight feet wide by five feet high. Players need not understand the importance of switching goals at halftime because there is no halftime.

The rules of the game are intentionally very simple so that the players can concentrate on the new skills and movement concepts they have learned instead of being burdened with remembering names of positions and numerous rules.

Start the game with a kickoff and use a kickoff after either team scores a goal. If a team kicks the ball out-of-bounds over the touchline, the opposite team receives a throw-in opportunity. If either team kicks the ball over the end line, the team whose goal is on that line gets a free kick. The nonkicking team must retreat to the half-field line, wait for the opposing team to kick the ball, and then pursue the ball. This is a variation of the traditional rules for corner kicks and goal kicks. There are no goalkeepers in this game. This allows the teams to score many goals, reduces collisions, and diminishes injuries.

In front of the goal is a safety zone, similar to a goal box, that no one may enter unless the ball is there. Then either team may enter.

This rule allows the offense to finish a play and the defense to stop a scoring opportunity, but it prohibits the defense from camping in front of the goal. The game includes no offside rules or penalty kicks, and all penalties result in a free kick from the spot of the foul. To get the best results with this, have six players on the field and six players on the sidelines. The six on the field play for five to seven minutes; then the six who were on the sidelines switch with the field players. Children this age need a break after five to seven minutes of continuous motion. The three-versus-three allows for continuous motion with hundreds of opportunities for collection and distribution. It also allows for numerous goal-scoring opportunities. The duration of the game should be approximately 30 minutes.

During the game, you should emphasize concepts like collecting, looking, and making a decision; support and balance; and recovering and depth on defense.

Collecting, Looking, and Decision Making

The three-versus-three game offers hundreds of opportunities to touch the ball. With only three players from each team on the field, players will often have the time and space to implement the process of collection and distribution—collecting, looking, and decision making. The coach should be on the field with the players encouraging them to use this process. Initially, the players will engage in a kick-and-run style. With patience and the application of this process, the game will begin to have more structure, and players will demonstrate better usage of space when in possession of the ball. Coaches should allow some time in the game for the players to play without their guidance.

Support and Balance

Players should be familiar with the activity monkey-in-the-middle drill (drill 49). To be successful in the monkey-in-the-middle game, the team in possession must always have two players in support positions. Instead of the players running to the person with the ball (closed space), they move to a support position (open space). The player who has collected the ball must then decide where the open space is and pass the ball. This is the beginning step in understanding the concept of triangulation. Players should then apply this knowledge to the three-on-three game. Encourage players whose team is in possession of the ball to move to open space in support positions rather than moving to the ball. As in the monkey-in-the-middle drill, after the player passes the ball, he must then move to a new support position. Continue to reinforce the concept of movement both with and without the ball. Encourage the players to make fat triangles, not flat ones (see figure 6.1). Fat triangles look like big triangles where players are able to support each other at angles of at least 45 degrees. Flat triangles look more like triangles that are trying to become straight lines. Fat triangles give depth in support. The passes made by players in flat triangles are very susceptible to being intercepted. Insure that players forming these triangles are balancing the field to spread the defensive players and discourage

Figure 6.1   Fat triangles (a) provide better support than flat triangles (b).

clustering. An easy method of explaining support and balance is to tell the players that the game is nothing more than a giant game of monkey-in-the-middle.

Recovering and Depth on Defense

Most young players want the ball so they can score goals. Sometimes, after the opponent has thwarted an offensive opportunity, players want to stand around and wait for someone else on their team to play good defense, get the ball, and pass it back to them so they can have another opportunity to score. Remember, in the three-on-three game, there is no offside rule, so this is a real possibility. Because there are only three players on each team, however, you should insist that all players recover to the goalside of their opponents. Explain to the players that the first rule of defense is for defenders to position themselves between their goal and their opponent. Generally, the offensive players are trying to find ways to invade the space behind the defenders. Depth in defending won't permit that. Coaches should explain depth in defending the same way that they explain depth in support when attacking. Flat triangles in defense will allow for penetrating moves and through passes. When the defense uses fat triangles instead, they limit the offensive opportunities because it is easier for them to recover.

Three-Versus-Three Plus Goalkeeper

This is the same three-versus-three, small-sided game with the addition of the goalkeeper. The goalkeeper is not allowed to come outside the safety zone, and no player is allowed inside the safety zone even if the ball is inside the zone.

Use this game with children five to seven years old who have had a year's experience with the three-versus-three. In some cases, where player combinations mandate mixing beginning players and players with prior experience, you may want to add the goalkeeper halfway through the season.

The goalkeeper adds new dimensions to the game. The attack must not only penetrate the defense but also beat the goalkeeper. The defense must reckon with the transition game after the goalkeeper collects the ball and initiates the attack. Give everyone who wants to experience the goalkeeper position a chance to do so. Not all children will want the opportunity because of the fear factor. Do not insist that these children play in the goal.

Teach only basic goalkeeping skills at this level. You should teach players to get their bodies behind their hands whenever possible, to catch and hold whenever possible, and to position themselves at the proper angle to reduce the space from which the attacker can shoot.

Seven-Versus-Seven

Use the seven-versus-seven game for players 8 to 10 years old. Play this game on a field approximately 70 yards long by 40 yards wide. Goals are approximately 6 feet high and 12 feet wide. Each team has six field players and one goalkeeper. Begin to use more structure at this level so that you can achieve more advanced outcomes. Assign players to teams and apply regulation rules. Establish the role of each player for kickoffs, throw-ins, goal kicks, corner kicks, free kicks, and penalty kicks.

The addition of more players will challenge the players' ability because they will have less time and space for decision making.

Team formations and player positions add more structure to the game. Defensive concepts that you should introduce or expand at this level include individual defensive principles, team defensive principles of help-side/ball-side defense, and compactness. Introduce or expand offensive principles such as support, width, ball possession in relation to thirds of the field, team formations, and set plays. These offensive and defensive principles are not original ideas, of course; they are borrowed from the traditional 11-versus-11 game.

Individual Defense

Teaching individual defense is difficult until players realize that each of them is responsible for defending either a space or a player or a combination of the two. Earlier training in the three-on-three games provides the necessary experience to understand this concept.

Once the player realizes his individual defense assignment, he should use the basic concepts of individual defense to accomplish his task. The first rule of individual defense is to stay goalside of the opponent. From this position the defender is able to deny his opponent space to the goal. If the opponent is in possession of the ball, the defender should force him to the outside, toward the sidelines, where he will be unable to shoot or make penetrating runs or passes. If the opponent collects the ball with his back toward the goal, the defender should prevent him from turning to shoot or pass by quickly challenging for the ball.

If the opponent has collected the ball and is already facing the goal, the defender will want to close the distance to the opponent quickly, assuming he has good defensive support and is not in a delaying action waiting for the defense to recover. In doing so, the defender should make a bending run toward the opponent to deny a passing lane or shooting opportunity. He should stop approximately four or five feet from the opponent and assume a defensive stance with legs slightly bent and arms slightly extended to aid in balance. The defender will then pressure the opponent away from the middle of the field toward the sidelines. When doing so, the defender will have one foot slightly behind the other and use sliding steps rather than crossing the feet. If the opponent changes directions, the defender uses a swing step to recover.

The second rule of individual defense is always to watch ball and player. To do this efficiently, the player should position himself where he has a clear picture of both. Sometimes this will mean retreating and giving up space rather than turning his back to the opponent and losing sight of him.

If the opponent is in possession of the ball, then seeing ball and player is no problem. If the opponent does not have the ball, the defender should position himself by considering the position of the opponent relative to the ball, the field position of the opponent, and how well he matches up athletically with the opponent. Generally, the defender should give more space to the opponent who has better speed and quickness.

Help-Side/Ball-Side Defense

The help-side/ball-side defense is a combination of zone and player-to-player defense. In this team defensive scheme, players have a responsibility to play the ball sometimes and passing lanes other times. This requires that players understand their position on the field in relation to the ball. Very simply, if their opponent has the ball then their responsibility is one of individual player-to-player defense. If their opponent is on the same side of the field as the ball, then they defend the opponent but are ready to give help if a team member gets beat by an opponent with the ball. This is called ball-side defense. If the ball is on the opposite side of the field, the defender moves to a position where she can provide cover and depth. This means there will be more space between the defender and the opponent she is marking. This should not be a problem as the defender will be able to recover to good defensive position by the time the opponent plays the ball to her side. This is called help-side defense. If the ball is in the middle of the field, then defenders play both sides of the field in a help-side manner.

Figure 6.2 shows an imaginary line drawn through the middle of the field. Players A and D are on the ball side while players B, C, E, and F are on the help side. Defensive players on the ball side, closest to the ball, should pressure the ball. Pressuring the ball will take time and space away from the attacker and may force her to make mistakes. When challenging the ball, the defender on the ball side should make a bending run toward the attacker. This will help to maneuver the attacker into less critical space while closing down a passing lane. Help-side defenders are ready to "help" if a defender is beaten.

The help-side/ball-side concept requires the defense to react as a team to the position of the ball. It is designed to deny critical space in the middle of the field.

Figure 6.2   An example of help-side/ball-side defense.

Compactness

The compactness theory of team defense helps insure balance to the defense and is relatively easy to understand.

During transition, when a team loses possession of the ball, the defenders should recover toward their penalty area. Having defenders recover in this manner will allow for compactness near the penalty area, which is critical space. As the players assume defensive positions farther away from the penalty area, they can use more spacing.

Their line of recovery should be in a V shape with the lines extending from the middle of the penalty area to the intersection of the midfield and sidelines. The defense should constantly employ concepts of help-side/ball-side and individual defense. The compactness concept helps to balance players so that they can use these strategies more effectively. With consistent use of this concept, players begin to realize that the closer they are to their goal, the more they should seal the middle of the field. The farther away from their goal, the less compactness the defense requires.

In the initial stages of teaching the concept of compactness, use lines of markers so the players can visualize the V and where to position themselves along the line of recovery. Their position in the line of recovery will depend primarily on the position of the ball.

Support

Do not designate players as either offensive or defensive players. Many times, young players practice only offensive techniques and tactics if they are designated as offensive players. The opposite is true, of course, if they are designated as defensive players. All players need to believe that they have both offensive and defensive responsibilities. There should be a team attitude that each player is a total player capable of scoring when the opportunity presents itself or coming up with a big play defensively if that's what the situation dictates.

Some coaches tell their defenders never to cross the midfield line for fear it would weaken the defense. These coaches also do not want their offensive players to recover to the defensive third of the field because it might affect a fast-break opportunity when they regain possession of the ball. If a defender never crosses a midfield line, then it becomes impossible for that player to get in a support position in the offensive third of the field. Maintaining possession of the ball during forward movement thus becomes difficult.

When coaches deny players the opportunity to make switching runs, they diminish or eliminate creativity and mobility in the attack. Instead, coaches should teach players to play as a unit. They should move in harmony using the help-side/ball-side concept. Keys to determining how well a team does with the support concept are the consistency with which they use good short, flat passes and how long they maintain possession of the ball.

To help develop the support concept in practice, coaches may want to interject one of these requirements in their scrimmages: (a) each time the ball crosses the midfield line, it must go back behind the midfield line again before it can be advanced; (b) no one may shoot until everyone has touched the ball at least once after it crosses midfield; or (c) no one may shoot unless everyone is on the offensive half of the field.

Width

The concept of width during support in attacking is an offensive tactic that players at the seven-versus-seven level should begin to incorporate in their game strategy. When players use the width of the field to generate an offense, the defense spreads more and is less compact in their defensive third of the field. The defenders must choose between defending the width, which allows for passing lanes, or compacting the defense and allowing passes to the outside. To help develop the concept of width during scrimmages, coaches can establish safe areas near the touchlines where no defenders are allowed. Because there is no defensive pressure in this area, players will be more inclined to pass to teammates occupying these spaces. Another way to develop this concept is to place minigoals on the touchlines that players may use to score. Use these during scrimmages, and players will be very willing to get the ball to the outside in both the offensive and defensive thirds of the field. Another method of encouraging players to play the ball wide is to prohibit defenders from defending wing players in possession of the ball until they reach the penalty area of the opponent.

Ball Possession

Ball possession is critical to the success of any team. If an opponent does not have the ball, she can't score. So the longer a team is in possession of the ball, the less chance the other team has to score. A factor that affects ball possession is the position of the player on the field and the risk factor associated with that position. You should encourage players in possession of the ball in the defensive third of the field to make swift decisions to move the ball out of that area. Loss of the ball in this area is critical. You should discourage ex-cessive dribbling or dangerous passes, particularly in the middle of the defensive third of the field. In this area it is generally more acceptable to make longer forward passes, even if not precise, or to intentionally kick the ball over the touchline, rather than risk loss of possession, which could lead to a scoring opportunity for the opposition.

In the middle third of the field, encourage the players to risk loss of possession by making penetrating runs or passes. Occasional loss of possession in this area is not as critical because there is plenty of space to recover on defense.

In the offensive third of the field, let the players know that the more chances they take, the more they will score. Do not let your players develop any mental blocks about shooting. Encourage them to take on defenders with their individual moves and to be aggressive in shooting. Loss of the ball in this area of the field will not be critical as players will have sufficient time to recover defensively.

Team Formations

Team formations provide the opportunity for coaches to identify a method for spacing players on the field with considerations for balance, cover, depth, and support. Give names to player positions to help communicate assignments to players.

The identification of these positions should not limit the movement of the players. Just because you designate a player to be the right wing attacker doesn't mean he has to stay on the right side of the field for the entire game, thereby stifling his creativity in movement. What it does mean, however, is that by designating or identifying a position, you expect someone to be there so that the team maintains field balance.

The number of field players in the seven-versus-seven game limits the variety of formations somewhat. Those that seem most popular are the 2-2-2, 3-1-2, and 3-3 formations.

The 2-2-2 formation, with two defenders, two midfielders, and two attackers, provides good balance. This system develops an understanding of linkage between defenders, midfielders, and attackers that players will use in later years in an 11-player system. The drawback of this system is that a team is weak in support or cover, which leaves them very vulnerable to counterattack.

The 3-1-2 system provides for three defenders, one midfielder, and two attackers. This formation will also help develop an understanding of the linkage concept between defenders, midfielders, and attackers. This system provides strong defensive depth. Its weakness is that it does not provide a numbers advantage in the attacking third of the field and is particularly weak in the midfield. Strong one-on-one efforts or switching runs often initiate scoring opportunities.

The 3-3 system may be the easiest to teach to beginning players with a background of only three-versus-three play. This system provides for good depth on defense and support in attacking. It is not difficult to explain support concepts using this system. Defensively, you can easily introduce lines of recovery and ball-side/help-side defensive concepts. The weakness of this system is that it does not provide for a three-tier linkage system.

Set Plays

You should introduce set plays at this level. This is another way the game begins to acquire more structure. When creating these plays, strive for simplicity. Complicated patterns of movement will only frustrate beginning players. Coaches should be cognizant of their players' abilities and design plays that their players can execute successfully.

Game situations that will dictate the need for creating and defending set plays include kickoffs, corner kicks, goal kicks, direct free kicks, indirect free kicks, penalty kicks, and throw-ins.

11-Versus-11

By the time the players reach 11 years old, they should be ready to continue their development playing on a regulation-size field approximately 110 yards long and 70 yards wide. The goals should be regulation—8 feet high by 24 feet wide. Apply official rules of soccer at this level.

You should continue to review and refine skills and concepts initiated at earlier levels. New concepts you should present at this level include more advanced individual skills, using space more creatively, systems of play for 11 players, set plays using more players, and linkage.

Individual Skills

At this level, the individual skills that you should emphasize include long passing, heading, and individual moves with the ball.

The players' size and strength will allow them to make long passes that were previously impossible. This ability will add a great deal of diversity to the attack. You should always encourage them to make the longest passes possible without jeopardizing possession of the ball.

Their ability to make longer passes will also enable them to change fields quickly, which can devastate help-side defenders. Long passing will enable them to cross the ball from the wing positions, thus developing the cross into a more dangerous offensive weapon. Heading is another skill that should receive more emphasis at this level. Players by now should have overcome any fear concerning heading. They should be aware that being able to head the ball with precision will allow them to maintain possession as well as increase scoring opportunities. The repertoire of individual moves for creating space with the ball should expand at this level. Players need to continue to explore ways to change direction, speed, and levels with the ball as well as develop a bag of tricks for themselves.

Goalkeepers should be increasing the level of their individual play. You should devote more practice time toward goalkeeping preparation with drills that emphasize speed and reaction time. More specifically, these drills should involve variations of catching, collecting, tipping, batting, diving, and clearing skills.

Using Space Creatively

Probably the most dramatic changes occurring at this level involve creative use of space without the ball, including the use of diagonal or vertical runs, horizontal runs, overlaps, switches, and takeovers. Diagonal or vertical runs are sprints that players use to create space for themselves to receive the ball. These runs are effective at this level because players now have the ability to make longer passes. This movement gives the defense something different to look at and thus causes confusion. Players generally make vertical or diagonal runs to create space for themselves and horizontal runs to create space for teammates.

You should incorporate into each practice session drills that emphasize using space more creatively. These drills should include two-player and combination plays involving more than two players. A two-player combination can be as simple as a player dribbling one direction and a teammate coming in from the opposite direction and taking the ball from him to continue dribbling (takeover). Another example of a two-player combination is a switch.

Figure 6.3 shows a simple switch that you can use as a finishing drill. After player A collects the ball in the corner, he can cross the ball to player B, who is making a run to goal for the shot. There are also combinations of movement using more than two players. Figure 6.4 shows player B passing to player A. Player C then runs ahead and outside player B to receive a pass from player A. This is a three-player combination using an overlapping run by player C. Figure 6.5 shows a four-player combination. After player C collects the ball, she can cross to player D, who is making a diagonal run to the goal.

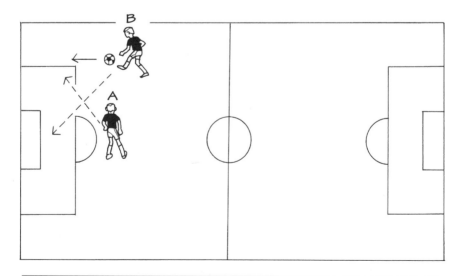

Figure 6.3   Basic switch drill.

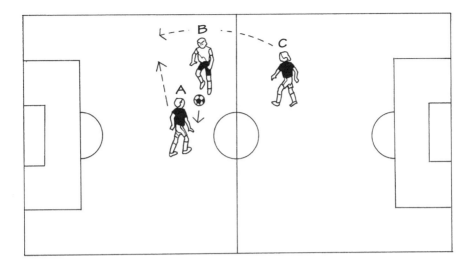

Figure 6.4   Three-player switch drill.

Figure 6.5   Four-player switch drill.

These are just a few examples of the drills you can use to initiate thinking about how to move more creatively. Coaches need to encourage players to keep proper field balance while moving more creatively, which is sometimes difficult with the 11-versus-11 scheme.

Play Systems

To add more structure to the 11-versus-11 game, coaches implement certain play systems or team formations. The system that a team uses will reflect the philosophy of its coaching staff. However, coaches need to select a system flexible enough to accommodate the strengths of their players. Coaches should not make the mistake of using a system that does not suit their players.

There are numerous systems from which coaches can select. The two that seem to be most suitable for players beginning at this level are the 4-3-3 and 4-4-2 systems.

The 4-3-3 system uses four defenders, three midfielders, and three attackers. The three midfield players support the four defenders. The midfield players have a dual role since they also support the attacking players. This formation creates numerous opportunities for natural triangulation that helps young players more easily develop a good short-passing game.

The 4-4-2 system uses four defenders, four midfielders, and two attackers. This system is a little more defense oriented. If you encourage midfielders to interchange positions and make supporting runs, your team will generate more offensive opportunities.

Linkage

Linkage is a term that describes the act of connecting passes in transition from defense to offense. Generally, midfielders are players who link the defense and offense; in some areas of the world midfielders are given the name links. The linkage process, then, is passing from defender to midfielder to attacker.

When moving from the 7-versus-7 game to the 11-versus-11 game, linkage becomes very important to the concept of intentional play.

In the 7-versus-7 game there were basically two tiers of players. In the 11-versus-11 formation, there is a third tier. This third tier of players creates natural triangulation and increases the passing possibilities on each possession. The third tier also increases the potential for switching, lateral runs, diagonal runs, and overlapping runs.

Coaches should emphasize the use of this linkage process from defender to midfielder to attacker so that play becomes more structured and intentional. Your team should form a balanced attack by combining this type of play—building the attack using linkage—with long passes from defenders to attackers making runs. A balanced attack, which combines both structured and fast-breaking styles of play, is difficult to defend.

Set Plays

The 11-versus-11 game creates a situation in which there are twenty players, excluding goalkeepers, on the field. Therefore, when designing set plays to create scoring opportunities, spacing should be a primary concern.

All players should understand their responsibility on each play. This will help insure that the team maintains proper spacing and does not become confused. The players at this level are bigger, stronger, and more highly skilled. Quick transition of the ball from one penalty area to the other is more likely.

Coaches should not make the mistake of making the team vulnerable defensively, particularly early in the game, by moving too many players forward in attacking positions during these free kicks.

In the defensive third of the field, all eleven players should contribute to the defensive effort. Sacrificing the attack by bringing them back on defense to regain possession of the ball and possibly prevent the opponent from scoring during free kicks is a sound defensive tactic.

Remember that the progression from the beginning player, age 5 through 7, to the player age 11 through 12 is a long process. Always be fair to the players by giving them helpful information that is appropriate for their current level of ability. Above everything, be patient through this process.

Using Drills in Practice

Practices should include a variety of drills, activities, small-sided games, and full-field games that will help promote the development of individual skills and concepts, group skills and concepts, strategies, and games. Use drills as an integral part of practices to develop a smaller part of the big picture. Drills enable the players to focus on one dimension without being distracted by having to concentrate on other aspects of the game.

Careful planning will allow coaches to use drills that are appropriate for the players and offer many opportunities for movement and touches on the ball. When planning, coaches should use drills to address specific areas of development. For example, if a team is having trouble scoring after moving the ball successfully to their offensive third of the field, then practices should include drills that emphasize finishing skills.

Making Practice Drills Successful

There are several key factors in making drills work successfully in practice. These include dividing the group into smaller parts, changing activities frequently, having sufficient equipment, varying formations, switching the order of activities, and making the drills gamelike.

Whenever possible, divide the players into small groups during drills. By using grids you can identify boundaries of general space for each group. In spacing grids consider safety and your ability to observe adequately. Small groups of players within these grids will have opportunities for hundreds of touches on the ball during each practice.

It is also a good idea to change combinations of players frequently so that everyone gets a chance to play with each other. Having small groups means players will become more accomplished in shorter periods of time because there is less standing around. Coaches will also have the opportunity to present more activities during each practice session. Generally spend no more than 10 to 15 minutes on a drill during each session. Changing drills frequently will help players stay motivated, which will increase their work rate. You must have sufficient equipment to implement drills with smaller groups. Ideally, there should be a couple dozen small-game markers of various colors, scrimmage vests, and a ball for each player in each team's equipment inventory. Along with regular goals, small, portable, temporary goals are helpful for drills.

Switching the order of activities occasionally will also help to make drill work go more smoothly. For example, players can work on a drill involving individual moves the first part of the first three practice sessions. On the fourth practice session, you could start practice with a small-sided, three-versus-three game and follow with drills that help develop individual moves. Breaking practice routines will keep players motivated.

Changing formations regularly will also give a different look to drills. Alternately using triangles, squares, and circles for drill work adds variety. Varying the number of players, number of balls, and amount of space for drill work will help to promote a high work rate.

Probably the single most important factor in the success of a drill is whether or not the players are having fun. Drills will be fun for players if you present them in a gamelike fashion. Many of the drills in this book have these gamelike qualities. Using them in their proper progression not only helps players develop skills and concepts but also is enjoyable for them.

Practices
for Five- to Seven-Year-Old Players

Practices for five- to seven-year-old players should last approximately 60 to 75 minutes. Each practice should include a variety of drills, activities, and small-sided games that will promote the development of individual skills and concepts, group skills and concepts, strategies, and games. At this level, offensive skill and concept development is much more difficult than defensive development. Therefore, when organizing your practice plan, design drills that have no defensive pressure or passive defensive pressure. While planning, always give the numbers advantage to the offense if there is a numbers differential, three-versus-one for example.

Develop a warm-up plan for your players. Follow this plan as players are arriving to practice. Include in the warm-up plan activities that involve various skills including juggling, passing, dribbling, heading, and shooting. Players can do these activities without much coaching instruction. The players will tend to gravitate toward the shooting station. Encourage them to spend equal time at all the stations. Before allowing players to go to stations, have them complete a warm-up and stretch for about 10 minutes. Have them warm their muscles by doing a sustained large muscle activity for 2 to 3 minutes followed by a stretching exercise. When stretching, use static stretching by slowly reaching a point of tightness, then holding that point. Avoid ballistic or bounce-type stretching. After a vigorous practice, encourage players to take a cool-down jog and stretch similar to the warm-up.

I recommend that at this level you use the three-versus-three or three-versus-three-plus-goalkeeper format for scrimmages. It's helpful to paint the goals different colors, for example, red and green. During the game have one team wear green jerseys, the other red. The painted goals give the players a visual cue in helping to determine direction. If other groups use the goals and painting is not allowed, simply tie a couple of green shirts to the top of one goal and red shirts to the other. If the teams switch sides at a specified time, simply untie the shirts and place them on opposite goals. If a player or players on the team are color blind, use shirts with symbols.

You should not place players in this age group on regular teams. Regular teams mean competition. When competition is emphasized

SAMPLE PRACTICE PLANS: FIVE- TO SEVEN-YEAR-OLDS

Type of activity	Content	Time
Large-group instruction	Moving vision drills (#7): level 1, 2	5 min
Large-group instruction	Stretch	5-7 min
Individual	Fancy-footwork drill (#20)	10 min
Partner	Partner tag (#24)	10 min
Partner	Thread-the-needle drill (#34)	5 min
Small group	Three-versus-three	20 min
Large group	Closure and cool-down stretch	5-10 min

Type of activity	Content	Time
Large-group instruction	Stationary vision training with a ball (#6)	10 min
Large-group instruction	Stretch	5-7 min
Individual	Fancy-footwork drill (#20)	10 min
Small group	Good-bye drill (#36)	10 min
Small group	Three-versus-three	20 min
Large group	Closure and cool-down stretch	5-10 min

Type of activity	Content	Time
Large-group instruction	Freedom drill (#22)	10 min
Large-group instruction	Stretch	5-7 min
Partner	Partner stationary shooting drill (#62)	10 min
Small group	Hello drill (#38)	10 min
Small group	Three-versus-three	20 min
Large group	Closure and cool-down stretch	5-10 min

too early, the development of skills and concepts is minimized. Coaches should view competition for five- to seven-year-old children like flu medication. If given in proper doses, it will be helpful. If given in too large a quantity, it can be harmful.

Each week when meeting with the players, divide the children differently so they experience playing with all the other children. On this and the preceding page there are three examples of how you should organize a typical practice for five- to seven-year-old children including stretching after warm-up activities.

Practices for 8- to 10-Year-Old Players

Practices for 8- to 10-year-old players should be approximately 75 to 90 minutes in duration. These players should have had previous experience playing three-versus-three and three-versus-three plus a goalkeeper.

Introduce team formations at this level. The game will have more structure and play should be intentional. Therefore, practice should continue to emphasize the process of collecting, looking, and decision making. You should introduce and reinforce individual and team defensive concepts of help side/ball side and compactness. At this level emphasize offensive principles like support, width, ball possession, and set plays.

One of the most difficult concepts to teach players at this level is how to deny space efficiently. Very often players at beginning levels feel it is their responsibility to defend the entire field. These players will follow any space the ball goes to. If there is an entire team of this type of player, there will likely be a swarming effect during play. To alleviate this situation, players must become aware of position on the field and how it relates to other positions.

SAMPLE PRACTICE PLANS: 8- TO 10-YEAR-OLDS

Type of activity	Content	Time
Large-group skillwork	Freeze drill (#23)	10 min
Large group	Stretch	5-10 min
Large group	Return-to-sender drill (#43): level 1	10 min
Small-group skillwork	Shake-and-take drill (#27): level 1	10 min
Large-group instruction	Explain team formation	15 min
Large-group game	Seven-versus-seven	20 min
Large-group instruction	Closure and cool-down stretch	5-10 min

Type of activity	Content	Time
Large-group instruction	Warm-up jog & stretch	10 min
Individual	Fancy-footwork drill (#20)	8 min
Small group	Circle dribble tag (#26)	7 min
Small-group skillwork	Monkey-in-the-middle drill (#49)	10 min
Small-group instruction	Run-and-shoot drill (#65)	10 min
Large group	Explain help-side/ball-side defense	15 min
Large-group game	Seven-versus-seven	10 min
Large-group instruction	Closure and cool-down stretch	5-10 min

Type of activity	Content	Time
Individual instruction	Fancy-footwork drill (#20)	10 min
Large group	Stretch	5-7 min
Small group	Pendulum drill (#40)	10 min
Partner	Partner heading drill (#56)	5 min
Small-group instruction	Pass-and-shoot drill (#67)	15 min
Large group	Explain using width of field	10 min
Large-group game	Seven-versus-seven	20 min
Large-group instruction	Closure and cool-down stretch	5-10 min

Coaches should continue to develop the skills and concepts that players should have learned at the five- to seven-year-old level. If players do not possess these skills or understand the concepts, coaches should not proceed until they establish a suitable foundation or offer an alternative for additional training.

On pages 204 and 205 there are three sample practice plans for 8- to 10-year-old players.

Practices for 11- to 12-Year-Old Players

Practices for the 11- to 12-year-old players should last approximately 90 minutes. You should continue to develop and refine the players' individual skills and concepts. The physical changes in the players (size, speed, strength) present new strategic opportunities. Practices will include exploring creative solutions that adapt a more mobile approach to attacking the opponent's goal. This mobile

SAMPLE PRACTICE PLANS: 11- TO 12-YEAR-OLDS

Type of activity	Content	Time
Individual instruction	Fancy-footwork drill (#20)	10 min
Large group	Stretch	5-10 min
Small group	Partner dribble game (#29)	10 min
Small group	Three-versus-three	10 min
Small group	Four-corner passing drill (#44)	7 min
Small group	Cat-and-mouse shooting drill (#75)	10 min
Large group	11-versus-11	20 min
Large-group instruction	Closure and cool-down stretch	5-10 min

Type of activity	Content	Time
Large group	Moving vision drills (#7)	10 min
Large group	Stretch	5-7 min
Small group	Check out-check in drill (#51)	10 min
Small group	Short and long heading drill (#57)	5 min
Small group	Come-and-get-me shooting drill (#76)	10 min
Large group	Explain system of play	15 min
Large group	11-versus-11	25 min
Large-group instruction	Closure and cool-down stretch	5-10 min

Type of activity	Content	Time
Individual	Fancy-footwork drill (#20)	10 min
Large group	Stretch	5 min
Small group	Three-versus-one shooting drill (#74)	15 min
Small group	Three-corner heading drill (#59)	5 min
Small group	Three-versus-three	15 min
Large group	Explain three-tier linkage	15 min
Large group	11-versus-11	20 min
Large-group instruction	Closure and cool-down stretch	5-10 min

approach will include flexibility in the positioning of players, introducing more complex concepts of width and support, and initiating new movement concepts. These new movement concepts will involve the value of switching runs, lateral runs, diagonal runs, and takeovers in attacking soccer.

Before you can present these new opportunities, you should make certain that players have learned the skills and concepts at the 5- to 7-year-old and 8- to 10-year-old stages of development. If this system has not been in place, go back as far as necessary in the development of skills and concepts to insure that your players have a positive experience while learning. On pages 206 and 207 there are three examples of practice plans for 11- to 12-year-olds. Remember, these practice plans are just a sampling of the variety of experiences available for 11- to 12-year-old players.

The plans include time for an 11-versus-11 scrimmage. Restricted team size often means that you will not have enough players for 11-versus-11. A possible solution to this problem is practicing with another team. You may even want to vary your schedule so you practice with several different teams.

Whichever age group you work with, try to remember that the players will spend considerably more time in practice situations than in games. Make the practices valuable, fun learning experiences that will keep kids coming back to enjoy another day of soccer with their friends.

About the Author

Jim Garland has worked with children ages 5 to 11 as an elementary physical educator for more than 26 years. He also has over 10 years' experience coordinating summer soccer camps and clinics for Motion Concepts Soccer Camps and has coached soccer teams, from beginners to high school age.

As an undergraduate at Towson State University, Maryland, Jim earned Most Valuable Player awards for two consecutive years. In 1970, he was elected Senior Athlete of the Year. In 1985 he was inducted into the Towson State University Athletic Hall of Fame. Jim earned his master's from Morgan State University, Baltimore, Maryland.

Jim is a member of the National Soccer Coaches Association of America, and the American Alliance for Health, Physical Education, Recreation and Dance.